Advance Praise for *Jews and Booze*

"I have had the privilege and pleasure of Michael Levin's heartfelt friendship for three decades. Michael's knowledge base, understanding, compassion, and dedication to people in recovery, especially in the Jewish community, is outstanding. You can trust his guidance."

—Rabbi Naftoly Bier, Rosh Kollel, Boston Kollel

"Often that which is most difficult to hear, is most important to hear. In his erudite and clear style, Michael Levin helps open our eyes to the difficult reality of addiction in the Jewish community. This book is a must read and critical resource for Rabbis (across the religious spectrum), lay leaders and anyone who desires to help those suffering from addiction."

—Rabbi Ari Zahtz, Congregation Bnai Yeshurun

JEWS
AND
BOOZE

Alcoholism, Addiction, and Denial in the Jewish World

MICHAEL LEVIN

WICKED SON

A WICKED SON BOOK
An Imprint of Post Hill Press
ISBN: 978-1-63758-536-8
ISBN (eBook): 978-1-63758-537-5

Jews and Booze:
Alcoholism, Addiction, and Denial in the Jewish World
© 2022 by Michael Levin
All Rights Reserved

Cover Design by Tiffani Shea

Post Hill Press
New York • Nashville
posthillpress.com
wickedsonbooks.com

Published in the United States of America
1 2 3 4 5 6 7 8 9 10

To David A., of blessed memory

TABLE OF CONTENTS

"The survivors only came out of the camps just once.
Alcoholics and addicts have to come out every morning."
—Rabbi Naftoly Bier, Rosh Kollel, Boston Kollel

FOREWORD

BY RABBI SHAIS TAUB

In Judaism, we often question ideas just to make them stronger. So I would like to be frank about my own question as to why I am writing a foreword to this book. To be sure, the author has done a masterful job at formulating and arguing his thesis. I am even quite sure it will save lives. But it is still not without hesitation that I go along with the idea that I be the one to introduce the reader to this book.

You see, as a rabbi who sometimes speaks and writes about recovery from alcoholism and addiction, I have taken great pains to avoid addressing the topic of alcohol abuse in any way and in any forum; and it is exceedingly important to me that I maintain that policy. I understand that this position tends to confuse people, so I will explain that which for me is an absolutely critical distinction. But I will need to do so in two phases.

The first point to be made is that while drinking has certainly destroyed countless lives through the ages, alcohol itself remains perfectly kosher. In Jewish mystical terms, alcohol is a neutral energy that can be sanctified through proper use or profaned through improper use. So God created alcohol for a purpose and we need not vilify it even while there are those individuals for whom it is harmful in any form or amount. Consider that there are people with deadly peanut allergies and we do not rail against peanuts.

The foregoing encapsulates, I think, the Torah's attitude toward alcohol which should make apparent why I as a rabbi feel no need to speak disparagingly about drinking as a whole.

But this still does not explain my apprehension about writing the foreword to this book. After all, the author does not condemn all drinking, only the normalization of over indulgent drinking which the Torah surely also forbids. As stated earlier, alcohol may be sanctified or profaned. Surely the abuse of alcohol (wherever you decide to draw that line) would constitute in the Torah's eyes such a profanation and thus be proscribed. Why then should I as a rabbi hesitate to be associated with condemning something that the Torah forbids? But this brings me to my second point.

Conceding the fact that there is some form or degree of drinking that is prohibited by Torah, there are still many wrong and unhelpful ways to communicate that fact. And depending on who you are (or even who people so much as think you are) there may be no productive way at all for you to address the topic. You see, in order to effectively carry a message of recovery from alcoholism (at least to those who really need to hear it), the speaker must not be perceived as one who has an inherently negative feeling toward drinking. So it may be okay for other rabbis to speak about the dangers of overindulgence, but not this rabbi. Hence, over the years I have declined requests to speak out even against the most universally recognized alcohol-related problems such as teenage drunkenness on Purim. Others may be able to afford being associated with that kind of message but I cannot. Does Judaism have an opinion on irresponsible drinking? There is no area of life in which Torah does not offer us guidance. But I leave that for other rabbis to deal with. As a rabbinic voice of empathy and support for those who choose to identify as alcoholics and addicts, I must carefully guard myself from taking any position that would undermine my ability to be helpful, and in this regard, I have taken many of my cues from the world of recovery, particularly the approach of Alcoholics Anonymous.

From its inception, the modern recovery movement which began with the advent of Alcoholics Anonymous in America in the 1930s was never a temperance movement or even loosely allied with the temperance movements of the time. As anyone familiar with the history of this country is aware, in the early part of the 20th century, voices decrying the perceived evils of drinking made up a social cause powerful enough to lead to the passing of a Constitutional Amendment prohibiting alcohol. In stark contrast, A.A. took a decidedly neutral stance on the subject of drinking. The original text of A.A., the "Big Book," published in 1939, states clearly that members need not avoid gatherings where alcohol is served and that furthermore, may choose to keep alcohol in their homes to serve to non-alcoholic guests. A particularly important passage in the Big Book makes clear the reasoning behind this ambivalence toward drinking:

"We are careful never to show intolerance or hatred of drinking as an institution. Experience shows that such an attitude is not helpful to anyone. Every new alcoholic looks for this spirit among us and is immensely relieved when he finds we are not witchburners. A spirit of intolerance might repel alcoholics whose lives could have been saved, had it not been for such stupidity. We would not even do the cause of temperate drinking any good, for not one drinker in a thousand likes to be told anything about alcohol by one who hates it. (Alcoholics Anonymous, p. 102.)"

The reader should now be able to understand why my first thought was not to attach my name to this most worthy project.

But as I said, we Jews question ideas to make them stronger. So now that I have shared my question with you, I will share my answer.

Having made clear that I have no interest in the topic of alcohol use or abuse, I will tell you now why I am deeply grateful that a book like this finally exists and also why I think it needed to make its case exactly the way that it does.

The reality is that right now there is someone in your neighborhood, your congregation, your school's parent body, or your softball team who is dying from a completely treatable disease called alcoholism. It's a drawn out and gruesome process of mental, emotional, and bodily collapse that pulls whole families and even communities down with it. It's maddening to so much as stand near it, let alone play any part in it. I don't believe there are words to sufficiently express how absolutely cursed it is but hateful and pitiful are the best I can manage. And among the most hateful and pitiful things about this consummately hateful and pitiful thing is that, for heaven's sake, it's completely treatable. You could scream. For the love of all that's holy. It's completely treatable. The only "catch" is that in order to treat it, the sufferer must acknowledge the illness and seek help. And therein lies the hatefulness and pitifulness. One of the main symptoms of this disease is that it is a disease that tells you that you don't have a disease.

It's part of the pathology. An alcoholic will use any argument to reason away their problem, often employing deft arguments that would make even the most seasoned Talmudic scholar's head spin. The sheer brain power of alcoholic rationalization is astounding—twisted and perverse but astounding. As I was told by an old timer in AA, "You know what it means to rationalize? Rational-lies." And it is this capacity to rationalize that makes a treatable condition so fatal.

You see, alcoholism isn't just a physical allergy to alcohol that causes an abnormal bodily reaction of craving more and more alcohol. If only it were a purely physical disorder the alcoholic could then avoid triggering it as easily as the one with the peanut allergy avoids an anaphylactic reaction by not eating peanuts. The blasted problem is that alcoholism is also a condition of the mind and one of its chief symptoms is self-deception. So the overwhelming odds are that someone you know and perhaps even care for is dying right now and making their loved ones' lives a living hell all because they continue to find reasons to convince themselves that they are not alcoholic.

And the Jewish alcoholic has one more excuse and ever present alibi to explain away their problem. "I can't be an alcoholic. I'm Jewish."

And when life finally becomes so painful as to force them to momentarily admit defeat, along comes the perfect reason why recovery is not an option. "I can't be in recovery. I'm Jewish."

So without condemning drinking, I think that we as a community have to ask ourselves if we wish to be party to perpetuating attitudes about Jewish drinking that will kill some of our friends and loved ones.

Is everyone who abuses alcohol an alcoholic? Certainly not. In my experience, most can and do stop when given sufficient reason to do so. It is only a small fraction of people who drink inappropriately that are real alcoholics in need of recovery—those who cannot stop even when it jeopardizes everything that is dear to them. But here's the thing. Even if it's just one person you know (and statistically speaking it's certainly more than just one person) who is fueling their self-deception by repeating a bunch of tired, old cultural myths about Jews not being alcoholics, don't you think at least one book should once and for all systematically deconstruct all of those harmful lies? Don't you think there should be at least one source that goes down the line and disabuses us of these notions one by one so that we can no longer deflect the truth that alcoholism can and does destroy Jewish families on a scale comparable to other communities? Shouldn't someone set the record straight about this for once?

I think so. And again, my reason is not because I have any opinion about the Kiddush clubs. I really couldn't care less about them. What I cannot countenance is that we as a community would create "plausible deniability" for the person who is dying a slow and entirely preventable death. Or that when they finally do consider the fact that they may need help, quickly dismiss the thought because treatment is somehow even less Jewish than the disease itself.

That's why I am so incredibly relieved that Michael Levin has taken on this task. I would never have done it myself. But now that someone finally did it, I believe that every responsible member of the Jewish community needs to at least know that this book exists. Not everybody will read this book. That's okay. But there needs to be a collective awareness that a comprehensive case has finally been set to writing proving that we Jews are not immune from alcoholism and that a culture normalizing alcoholism while stigmatizing recovery has particularly exacerbated that which is a universal problem.

I trust that those who read this book will find it easy and pleasant to read but quite difficult to live with. And that is as it should be. This book should disturb all of us until the culture changes enough that a book like this becomes outdated. What is a culture? People make up a culture. We change the culture by changing people, beginning with ourselves. Yes, alcoholics will always look for excuses, but let us not be able to say that the Jewish community served up those excuses on a silver platter. Choosing recovery is hard enough without the community collectively enabling. Instead, let's strive to be a model of healthy attitudes toward alcoholism and recovery. I do not think we will eradicate alcoholism until Moshiach comes, but until then we should be able to pride ourselves on creating a culture where those who need help are able to recognize it and get that help sooner.

Before I conclude, I would like to briefly mention a point that is separate from all of the above. The author makes a compelling argument that untreated emotional pain and trauma in multigenerational Holocaust families may also be an underlying cause of alcoholism and addiction. Although I am by no means qualified to evaluate such a statement, I find the idea fascinating and it rings rather true to me. I pray that this book might find the right audience who can see to it that this matter will be adequately addressed, not only by funding studies but more importantly by providing the expansion of desperately needed social services to families who suffer.

May we soon see the day when all suffering is but a dreamlike memory.

—Rabbi Shais Taub

WHY I WROTE THIS BOOK

His name was David. He came from a well-known and well-respected Flatbush family and he was my best friend.

And he died with a needle in his arm.

When it happened, I felt responsible for his death. He had overdosed on heroin (as if there's an appropriate "dose" for a drug like that) and he was found in his apartment one summer day several days after he had died. He left behind a wife and a beautiful daughter.

Why did I feel responsible? Because I'd seen the signs. His erratic behavior. His failure to attend minyan. His failure to answer the phone. I tried to talk with him about it, but he would always blow me off. He was a social user, he would tell me. He had it under control. He was fine.

And then one day, he wasn't fine.

For a full year, I blamed myself. Why couldn't I have gotten through to him? Why didn't I try to convince him to go to rehab, whatever that was? Why couldn't I have gotten him to see the damage he was doing in his own home and to his parents, friends, and community?

I later learned that given the true nature of addiction, I was powerless to interfere with his addiction, which I heard described as "suicide on the installment plan." There was nothing I could have said or done to prevent his death or even to slow his addiction. Over time, I learned to release the guilt.

But I couldn't let go of the loss.

In order to find some meaning in David's death, I was advised to study alcoholism and addiction and maybe find a way to help people who were in David's position, or in his wife's position. So I did. I read book after book, spoke to addicts and counselors, and attended open "12 Step meetings" where I listened to alcoholics and addicts tell their own stories.

I was hooked, no pun intended.

And for more than thirty years, I have served as a volunteer addiction counselor—not as my profession but as my avocation. As my *kapporah* or atonement. *Kapporah* for what exactly? For what I still consider my failure to act more decisively when I knew that David's life was circling the drain.

Over those decades, it has been my privilege to sit with addicts and alcoholics and help point them toward the path of recovery. I've also spent innumerable hours with parents, spouses, and siblings of addicts and alcoholics. I've shared with them what I've learned about what they can do to take care of themselves and what they can and cannot do for their loved ones still drinking or drugging.

I grew up in secular America and became observant while in college. So I've seen "both sides of the fence"—secular and religious Judaism—and I've seen addiction and alcoholism in both of those worlds. We Jews aren't any more or any less prone to addiction than our non-Jewish counterparts. But it's possible that we Jews, secular and religious alike, have a harder time than other people getting help.

The purpose of this book is not to point out some sort of scandal or to criticize anyone or any Jewish community. *Chas v'shalom*—Heaven forbid. Instead, I want to share with my fellow Jews what I learned after David's death. I want to "carry the message," as it's said in recovery-speak, about what addiction is, what alcoholism is, what recovery is, and what denial is. The goal is to reduce the unnecessary suffering that exists in our communities because of the twin scourges of alcoholism and addiction.

Maybe you know someone who's suffering—an addict, an alcoholic, a loved one. Maybe you want to help, or maybe you just want to understand what's really going on, so you can protect yourself.

This is the book I wish I could have read before David died.

Instead, this book is for you.

CHAPTER 1

The Star of David Syndrome

Ever hear someone say, "Jews aren't alcoholics or addicts! That's a Gentile thing!"

The belief that Jews are safe from addiction has pervaded our communities for longer than you can imagine. Even when addiction might be staring you in the face, we have our ways of brushing it under the rug. We could call the phenomenon of Jewish denial about addiction the "Star of David" syndrome. We somehow believe that being Jewish is a guard against drinking too much, eating too much, gambling too much, or indulging in inappropriate sexual relationships. Wherever we are on the religious spectrum, we don't believe Jews are capable of such things because of our superior culture or our religious observance.

Interestingly, there is another group that tends to deny that it has any issues. When it comes to addiction in general, it's often said that "the denial is bigger than the disease." In other words, most people with alcohol, drug, gambling, eating, or spending problems don't want to acknowledge those problems to themselves or to anyone else. As one of the key pieces of recovery literature states, "Who cares to admit complete defeat?"

Most alcoholics and addicts[1] tell themselves they can beat their "habit," that they aren't that bad, that they aren't *really* addicted, that they aren't hurting anyone but themselves or a variety of similar delusions. Addiction is unusual in that way—it's a disease no one wants to admit to having.

People diagnosed with cancer, heart ailments, liver problems, lung issues, and similar maladies don't tell their doctor, "You're wrong, I don't have that." They may be shocked, they may be frightened, or they may ask for a second opinion, but generally, when people are diagnosed with a life-threatening disease, they just want to know what they can do to overcome it.

Not so with addiction. The addictive life, however damaging it may be, is the normal life for the addict. To any rational person, drinking oneself to death, racking up huge credit card debt, eating to the point of obesity, or overeating and forcing oneself to throw up are insane choices to make. But to the addict, this is normal.

In the Jewish community, we have our own bad "habits" that we like to deny. We like to deny that any of our community leaders could be sex offenders. We like to deny that though we claim to be spiritually oriented, in some

---

[1]   We will use the terms "alcoholics" and "addicts" interchangeably. The distinctions between the two aren't significant for the purposes of the discussion in this book.

communities, image is everything. And perhaps, most importantly, we like to deny that addiction is with us, and with us in a big way.

As in other areas of life, our denial gives way to stigma—stigma against the few people who admit to or are known to have a problem. As a result, we reinforce our denial by hiding even more. Practically every individual in the Jewish community who has an addiction wants to hide it instead of acknowledging it, asking for help, and treating it. The fear of ostracism is so great that we would rather suffer in silence.

Families don't want to admit that a parent or child has a problem with alcohol or drugs or gambling or pain medicine or any other addictive behavior or substance. It's even worse in the Orthodox world, of which I am a member. That's because the social pressure to appear *heimish*[2] is so intense. An Orthodox Jewish doctor, a friend of mine, served at an Orthodox Jewish sleepaway camp. He told me that one camper had gone into a diabetic coma and was fifteen minutes from death when he was discovered. His parents had not informed the camp that the boy was a diabetic. When the doctor asked why (after he had saved the boy's life), the mother explained, "We didn't want word to get out in the community that he was diabetic. We were afraid of what people would say."

The world of *shidduchim* (or the Orthodox dating world) places so much pressure on families to present a "perfect" background that Orthodox Jews are rightly afraid that if they admit that a family member has a problem, the children won't be able to get married. One Orthodox man who

---

[2]   A hard-to-translate Yiddish term that essentially means "beyond criticism even by highly critical fellow Jews."

got sober was told he could no longer drive carpool, because of his drinking problem. Nobody had a concern about him driving kids when he was still drinking, and they all knew the open secret that he was a fall-down drunk. But once word got out that he was sober, he was kicked out of the carpool rotation. You can't make this stuff up. People are terrified if they tell the truth about their addictive behaviors, they will be shunned, thrown out of school, out of the community, or worse.

Why do addicts live in denial? One reason they won't admit the painful truth about themselves is because they are afraid they will be judged. Unfortunately, in many corners of the Jewish community, they will be judged—swiftly, harshly, and most likely permanently—with the stigma falling on their family members, too. While denial is a fundamental aspect of addiction for addicts and alcoholics of all religions, races, and socioeconomic backgrounds, it's an even worse situation for Jews.

It Comes Out in the End

Addicts often act as if they live in a bubble. They think that no one else can see what they're doing and that no one else knows that they're getting away with it. In reality, they may be getting away with things for a while, but eventually, the truth comes crashing down upon them. They turn up drunk, hungover, or fail to show up to a work commitment or a family or religious obligation. They eat so much they can't fit into their clothes. They leave a browser open. Or the paycheck never makes it from the workplace to the home because it got swallowed up along the way at the liquor store, the bar, the bookie joint[3], the drive-thru Krispy Kreme, or the crack house.

One of my friends used to take his young daughter with him when he went to downtown Los Angeles in the middle of the night to score drugs. He would raise the hood of his car so his daughter couldn't witness the transaction. And then he died—with a needle in his arm. His hiding came to nothing.

A heartbreaking article[4] in the *Atlanta Jewish Times* tells the devastating story of five young Jews in their twenties and thirties who died of heroin "overdoses" (as if there were a proper dose for heroin). They're all buried in the same cemetery, and the parents only met because the graves of the young people were in the same part of the cemetery. Sadly, this doesn't only happen in Atlanta.

A young Orthodox woman had four children with her husband before divorcing him for his total relapse into drug addiction. She later buried him, the father of those children, when he died of an overdose.

The truth comes out in the end. Our denial does not suppress reality; it only pressurizes it, so when it is eventually released, it hits our community with the force of dynamite. Every funeral of a teen, every funeral of a parent, every DUI that risks the lives of not only the driver but others on the road, every incarceration, every family whose father fails to be present because he is passed out drunk on the couch—will testify against us eventually.

---

[3] Now conveniently available online 24/7 for your gambling pleasure.
[4] Harrison, Leah R., "Trapped in Atlanta's Jewish Heroin Triangle." *atlantajewishtimes.com,* August 31, 2016, https://www.atlantajewishtimes.com/trapped-atlantas-heroin-triangle/

We Are Stopping Our Addicts from Stopping

Addiction is a lonely, painful, brutal, selfish way to live. The activity or substance that initially brought relief to the addict boomerangs on the user, causing absolute destruction to that person's reputation, family, school, or community. Not to mention the *din v'cheshbon*—the heavenly accounting—later on.

Given the high price of addiction, you would think most addicts would want to stop. And a lot of the time, they do. But how are they supposed to stop if telling the truth about themselves to a spouse, a loved one, a rabbi, or a *rosh yeshiva* (head of a Talmudic seminary) can so often lead to blame, hostility, ostracism, or even exile? In some Jewish communities, families with an addicted or alcoholic child ship him off to rehab—usually in another part of the country—and pretend he doesn't exist. It's like a Soviet-style "disappearance." That's what you can get for putting your hand up and saying, "I have a problem."

Under those circumstances, it becomes easier for the addict to keep on using, drinking, or acting out. In a community where the stigma of addiction is so huge, the guilt around having an addiction is compounded, fueling even more addictive behavior. At the same time, the fear of ostracism makes it nearly impossible to confess to a problem and seek help.

It's said that all alcoholics and addicts stop drinking or using. The lucky ones get to stop during their lifetimes. The unlucky ones end up like my LA friend with a needle in his arm, robbed and murdered when they go to score drugs, or humiliated because of a drunk driving arrest. To think that these things aren't happening in our community is to invoke a communal level of denial that far outstrips the denial practiced by any addict or alcoholic.

This is no way for us to live as a people.

This is no way for families to live.

This is no way for individuals to live.

Time to Tell the Truth

It's time for us to surrender the myth of the Star of David syndrome—the idea that being Jewish somehow protects us from the crises and catastrophes that addiction imposes on individuals, families, and communities.

We have to tell the truth about ourselves.

When it comes to alcoholism, drug abuse, impulsive overeating, impulsive spending, and the like, *we are prone to stumble like any other human being.*

On Yom Kippur, we sing the Ashamnu, as a community, and often quite loudly. We are rejoicing in our humanity, in our imperfections, and in our certainty that despite whatever bad things we might have done, a loving God will forgive us, will embrace us, and will help us to do better.

It's time to apply that same Ashamnu mentality to addiction. It's time for us to admit, out loud and as a community, that alcoholism and addiction are within our gates, within our yeshivas, within our synagogues, at our Shabbat tables, at our simchas, and behind closed doors. It's time to sing out, not mumble with excuses, that addiction exists in our community and actually thrives on the vow of silence we've taken to keep ourselves from telling the truth.

It's time to recognize addiction for what it is: *a disease, not a disgrace.* A series of behaviors that can be arrested, so that the addict or alcoholic can face the underlying causes and conditions that led to the addictive behavior, and thus live a productive, happy life, untempted by the substances and behaviors that could have killed him or her at any moment.

Only when we admit that the problem exists can we begin to save the lives of the addicts in our communities— and the lives of their spouses, children, parents, and families.

Our grandparents used to joke, "*Shiker iz a goy*," meaning that "only non-Jews can be alcoholics."

Sorry, Grandpa and Grandma.

Shiker is a Yid.

It's okay. There is a solution. And it starts by telling the truth, and the truth is what this book is about.

CHAPTER 2

The Book of Numbers

W as there ever a time when Jews didn't drink or didn't drink a lot? Maybe there was. Today, walking into the janitor's closet on a Shabbat morning to observe the Ritual Committee, or joining a weeknight Chabad farbrengen should be enough to convince you that drinking is with us—and with us in a big way.

Orthodoxy may consider itself above addiction, but it is actually mired in alcohol consumption. I speak from experience—I am Orthodox myself. In fact, if there were ever a community whose culture offered addiction the opportunity not just to grow but to flourish, it would be ours. A facile thing is to point a finger at every other religious, ethnic, and socioeconomic group and say that addiction is their problem, not ours. In truth, however, traditional Judaism is literally built on the use of wine and hard liquor.

The Book of Numbers: How Many Times a Year Do the Orthodox Drink?

Case in point—have you ever said or heard anyone say, "I never drink, unless it's connected to something Jewish?"

Many Jews who would never dream of considering themselves problem drinkers will often make a statement like this. They will tell you that the only times they touch alcohol is when the Torah commands it or when there's a Jewish life-cycle event at which alcohol is typically consumed. That sounds great in theory, but if you look at the Jewish calendar, you'll discover that there is a shockingly high number of events when it's "kosher" for Jews to drink. So I thought I'd do the math and try to determine how many times a Jew can legitimately drink alcohol in a religious setting without raising the eyebrows or ire of friends and loved ones.

The precise figure? Well, in Judaism, the answer is, as always, "It depends." But if you add everything up, you can legitimately take a drink in our faith anywhere from 268 to 332 times a year. That's nearly daily drinking! There are plenty of people who have gotten sober in Alcoholics Anonymous who never drank as often as Jews drinking when the Jewish calendar tells them to!

If you're curious how I arrived at that number, I'll break it down for you right here.

First, there's Shabbat—the weekly celebration that offers not one opportunity for consuming alcohol, but up to five opportunities over the course of twenty-five hours, for each of the fifty-two weeks of the year! Take a look at our Shabbat drinking opportunities over the course of a year.

- Friday night Kiddush: 52

- Shabbat morning Kiddush at shul: 52
- Shabbat day meal Kiddush: 52
- Havdalah: 52
- "Kiddush club" or Ritual Committee: 52
  =Shabbat total: 260 drinking opportunities/year

So now we're up to a staggering 260 drinking occasions a year. And "staggering" is exactly the right word. Anybody who drinks 260 times over the course of a 365-day calendar is *likely* to be staggering. But that's not all. Then, there's Yom Tov. When you add up the holidays of Pesach, Shavout, Sukkot, Shmini Atzeret, and Rosh Hashanah, it comes to twelve. Include Yom Kippur and you're at thirteen. And with the exception of Yom Kippur, each of these days has got the same opportunities for drinking as Shabbat.

- Yom tov evening Kiddush: 12
- Yom tov morning Kiddush at shul: 12
- Yom tov day meal Kiddush: 12
- Havdalah: 13 (because you do say Havdalah after Yom Kippur)
- "Kiddush club" or Ritual Committee: 12
  =Yom tov total: 61 drinking opportunities/year

Add that to our Shabbat total and you get 321 opportunities to drink. And that doesn't include l'chaims that people make on *Chol Hamo'ed*, the intervening days of a holiday—when Jews will often throw parties and celebrate with—you guessed it—more alcohol!

Now let's talk about life-cycle events. When Jews hatch, match, or dispatch, we do so with wine or other alcoholic beverages as part of the simcha. So, let's say that over the course of the year, you attend a fairly small number of such events. Let's call it two weddings, one *sheva brachot* (the dinners in the week after the wedding), one *brit milah* or circumcision, one pidyon haben, one bar mitzvah, one bat mitzvah, one funeral, and two yahrzeits. Why do I include yahrzeits? Because at morning services, the person saying kaddish often brings a bottle of booze. Everyone has a shot and says, "The neshama should have an aliyah."[5]

That's ten more times, at a bare minimum, when we open a bottle. So we're up to 331 times to drink—or a mere 267 times if you're not a member of the Ritual Committee.

And then, finally, lest we forget, there's Purim, which makes it 268. (Or, if you're on the Ritual Committee, 332.)

So the next time someone Orthodox tells you, "I don't have a drinking problem. All I do is drink when my religion commands me to," be skeptical. That individual may be drinking, on average, five or six times a week. That's a lot of booze, all sanctioned by our religion. When people think about alcohol and Judaism, they typically call to mind Simchat Torah and Purim, two holidays famous (or notorious) for big drinking. But those two *chagim* actually cover the real Jewish drinking schedule, which allows for those 268 alcohol opportunities each year.

Americans love to make fun of the French, who allegedly drink wine at every meal. Or the Germans or British, who

---

[5]   The older gentlemen at my synagogue in Manhattan preferred J&B Scotch for such purposes. They told me that J&B stood for "Jewish Booze."

drink beer as if it were bottled water. Maybe these groups consume lots of alcohol; maybe they don't. But we sure do.

Secular Jews, Wipe That Smirk off Your Faces

Secular Jews might take this opportunity to smugly look down on their skull-capped brethren, but they would be mistaken to do so. The point of the above calculation is to rebuff the myth that Orthodox Jewish culture is dry compared with a bar-going, binge-drinking secular society. But the levels of drinking in secular cultures are pervasive and very often toxic. Secular Jewish culture, by which I mean the life of any North American Jew who does not live on the calendar and clock of Orthodox Judaism, is just as saturated with alcohol as Orthodoxy, if not more so. The occasions and settings for drinking are different, but they're equally numerous. Don't kid yourself, my secular friend. Your world is just as shot through with booze as that of the Orthodox. Let me explain.

Don't Forget the "Bar" in Bar Mitzvah

The party starts in middle school when what is often the last point of contact with Judaism is attending bar and bat mitzvah celebrations.

Bar and bat mitzvahs these days, outside the Orthodox world, rival royal weddings in terms of pomp, circumstance, cost, and flow of booze. Indeed, as the expression goes, the bar is often bigger than the mitzvah. Whatever spiritual benefits may accrue to twelve- and thirteen-year-olds from attending bar and bat mitzvahs, the most important thing from their perspective is relatively easy access to alcohol. If you're thirteen and you cannot sneak drinks at a bar or bat mitzvah, you should be ashamed of yourself. It's easy to find, easy to get hold of, and easy to sneak past one's parents, who are getting liberally loaded at their own tables.

A Lifetime of Drinking

If only the bat and bar mitzvah were the end of the party rather than the beginning! We all know how alcohol continues to flow robustly for the next ten to twenty years of a teen and young adult's life, especially when participating in secular culture. From high school, where many kids have their antennae up at all times for ways to find alcohol and drugs, to college where parties encourage binge drinking, drug use, and so on.

The drinking continues beyond the fraternity parties at your alma mater, however. You graduate, somehow, and you enter the workforce. While the three-martini lunch might have vanished from our culture and Mad Men-style drinking at the office is no longer a thing, alcohol at work is never hard to find. Thursday night beer blasts. Friday afternoon beer blasts. Going out with the team after work, any night of the week. Softball on the weekends wouldn't be softball without beer and pizza afterwards. Dinner with clients? Time to buy a nice bottle of wine or three on the company credit card. And then there are holiday parties, which took a hit in the COVID era, but will be back in full swing once the pandemic is finally put to bed.

When we look at secular social lives, the song remains the same. How do you entertain yourself and others, whether there's a pandemic raging or not? Most socializing these days takes place in bars and clubs. It's hard to imagine not having a drink or seven when you're out with your friends at a nightclub or bar, whether it's down the street or on the Vegas Strip. Yet one more place where alcohol consumption is the norm in secular society.

Then, there's watching sports, which comes with its requisite six-pack (or more). Until recently, you could not advertise hard liquor on television. Today, rap stars, artists, and other celebrities have joined the bevy of attractive women and handsome men enjoying themselves with vodka, rum, scotch, beer, and lots of other good-looking people. The message: Hard liquor is fine, desirable, and socially acceptable. And then comes the nagging tagline, *drink responsibly*. But why would anyone want to do that, when drinking looks like so much fun?

Lifestyle events in the secular world are just as prone to alcohol misuse as those in the Orthodox world. What's a wedding without an open bar? What's a funeral without an open bar, for that matter? A recovered alcoholic I know told me about going to a wedding shortly after he'd stopped drinking. There came that moment where everything seemed to speed up when seemingly the entire party had reached "alcohol mach ten." The noise was noisier, the music was bouncier, the room was sweatier, and almost everybody was well along in their alcohol-induced buzz. He'd had enough, so he quietly made his way to the door. One of the larger friends of the groom saw him and stopped him.

"You can't go," he bellowed.

This was a fellow famous for getting loaded at weddings and smacking other people in the head with his large and powerful forehead. My friend was not happy to see him.

"What did you say?" my friend asked, afraid the guy would head-butt him for no particular reason.

"You can't go!" he said a second time. "You're not drinking! You're going to be our designated driver!"

My friend wasn't having it. *Thanks for noticing, but no thanks.* He left the wedding.

Yes, alcohol consumption is as pervasive in the secular world as it is in the Orthodox world—and for Jews participating in the former, they sometimes get the best of both. The Friday keggers, Saturday softball games a la Budweiser, the holiday parties at work, *and* the four cups of wine on Passover. L'chaim!

Ironically, the one place where secular Jews drink the least is at temple. There's almost something weird about having more than a sip of wine at a non-Orthodox service, whether we are talking about anything from Chavurah or Reconstructionist to Reform or Conservative. It just doesn't feel right to do that kind of drinking in that kind of sacred space. But not to worry. Secular culture offers enough opportunities that you don't have to worry whether you're going to drink at temple or not.

And we haven't even touched on the other addictions and habituations to which secular Jews, like Orthodox Jews, are so often beholden, such as eating disorders, drug addictions, and compulsive spending. With marijuana delivered legally to your doorstep with just a few clicks on a smartphone, don't tell me grass isn't a gateway drug.

Yes, however you spin it, Jews today are mired in booze and drugs. So how can we continue to be so blind to the misuse of drinking among us? Orthodox, secular, or somewhere in between, it's time for all of us to wake up and smell the mojitos.

16

CHAPTER 3

So How Did We Get So into Booze?

However you play it, Jews anywhere on the spectrum of observance live in cultures saturated with alcohol and overwhelmed with drugs. How did this happen? In fact, for a long time, the Jewish attitude that alcoholism and addiction are Gentile problems and not Jewish problems might have been true. Not today, but once upon a time.

Dr. Glenn Dynner, professor and chair of religion at Sarah Lawrence College, wrote a fascinating book about Jewish tavern owners in Poland from the 1600s to the early 20th century. In *Yankel's Tavern: Jews, Liquor, and Life in the Kingdom of Poland* (2013), Dynner traces the history of the relationship between Jews and Gentiles in Eastern Europe.

According to Dynner, leases on taverns were extremely lucrative for the Jews fortunate enough to own them. Jews entered the tavern trade because Polish landowners didn't want to give up the money they could earn from tavern-keeping. At the same time, they didn't want to run the taverns themselves. The solution seemed simple—hire someone to do the work for you! Interestingly, they preferred to hire Jews. The Gentile peasants were known to be drunkards, so the landlords reasoned that they might drink up all the profits. So landowners turned to Jews (who were also literate and good at math) to sell their alcohol.

Since taverns were money-spinners, Jews had to maintain the appearance of sobriety to keep their businesses alive. If they did drink excessively, they did so behind closed doors, at religious events, far from prying Gentile eyes. Hence was born not only the Jewish belief but the Gentile belief that Jews were more sober than their Gentile neighbors. And, perhaps, such was the case. Not only that, but Jews were proud of their supposed sobriety and conveyed as much in their writing and popular culture.

Consider Abraham Joshua Heschel's description of Polish Jews:

> There were many who lived in appalling poverty. Many were pinched by the never-ending worries and there were plenty of taverns available with strong spirits. But drunkards were almost never seen amongst Jews. When night came and a man wanted to while away his time, he did not hurry to the tavern to take a drink. He went rather to his books or joined a

*group that even with or without a teacher gave
itself over to the pure enjoyment of study.*[6]

Reading this description, as a Jew, evokes a certain feeling of pride in our tradition and restraint. We are a People of the Book, after all. We have no need to drown our sorrows in liquor! That same feeling of pride underlies the mocking attitude in the famous Yiddish song, *Shiker iz der goy*, which appears in the original and translated version below.

Original Yiddish	Mark Slobin translation
Geyt der goy in shenk arayn.	*The Gentile goes into the tavern.*
Tinkt er dort a gleyzele vayn.	*He drinks a glass of wine there.*
Oy, shiker iz der goy.	*Oy, the Gentile is drunk.*
Shiker iz er, trinken muz er	*He's drunk, has to drink,*
Vayl er iz a goy.	*Because he's a Gentile.*
Geyt der yid in bes-medresh arayn.	*The Jew goes to the House of Study.*
Kuket er dort in a seyfer arayn.	*He looks into a book there.*
Oy, nikhtern iz der yid.	*Oy, the Jew is sober.*
Nikhtern iz er, lernen muz er	*He's sober, he has to study,*
Vayl er iz a yid.	*Because he's a Jew.*[7]

---

6   Heschel, Abraham Joshua, "Introduction" from Vishniac, Roman, *Polish Jews: A Pictorial Record*, Schocken Books, 1947

7   Slobin, Mark. *Tenement Songs: The Popular Music of the Jewish Immigrants.* University of Illinois Press, 1996. Yanky Lemmer, cantor of Manhattan's Lincoln Square synagogue, sings it here: https://www.youtube.com/watch?v=hmhV5Xy4cAw

Yes, Jews have long glorified themselves in their supposed sobriety. And yet even among the tavern-running Jews of Eastern Europe, drunkenness was not as absent as it seemed.

Skeletons in the Closet

Elijah Guttmacher was a Jewish "miracle worker" in the 1870s or an individual who sought to improve life for Jews through prayer and spiritual means. A collection of letters that he received and sent are at the YIVO Institute for Jewish Research. This collection paints a picture for us of the emotional life of the Jews of Eastern Europe, including their inner struggles and needs. Painful accounts in these letters relate to that condition that was supposed to be absent—alcoholism— within the Jewish community.

In one account, a wife beseeches R' Guttmacher to pray for livelihood for her husband:

> And he is like a ship in the sea, "and there was a mighty tempest in the sea so that the ship seemed likely to be wrecked [Jonah 1.4]" If God does not have mercy and if the respected, the Admor does not arouse God's mercy so that he will now get another lease so that he can support himself. And for the prosperity of his body, for he is accustomed to cheer himself with cases of liquor. And he became ill from this with a dangerous weakness of the heart, may he have a speedy recovery.[8]

---

[8]   YIVO, RG 27, Elijah Guttmacher Collection, 314, Zawoda

Emotional turmoil and stress were unquestionably significant among Eastern European Jews, and with alcohol becoming cheaper to produce and so often under Jewish control, Jews almost certainly used it to drown their problems, as this story demonstrates.

Other evidence of addiction among Jews appears in the literature of the time. Sholem Aleichem, the writer whose *Tevye and His Seven Daughters* (or *Tevye the Dairyman*) became the basis for the musical *Fiddler on the Roof* (1964), wrote a story called "It Doesn't Pay to Be Good." The story tells of a Jewish man addicted to gambling, so much so that the heartache caused by his errant behavior killed his wife and left his daughter orphaned:

> *The boy was a bum! What do I mean by a bum? I mean he had a passion for cards. Why, passion isn't the word for it: cards were his be-all and end-all, he would have walked a hundred miles for a hand of them!*
>
> *At first it was just a round of sixty-six, or, once a month on a long winter night, a harmless game of challenge or klabberjass among friends...except that he began to play more and more—and with all kinds of riffraff, the worst loafers, drifters, and grifters. Take it from me, once a man starts with cards there's no telling where he'll end up.*
>
> *Who even thinks then of praying three times a day, or wearing a hat on his head, or observing the Sabbath laws, or anything else that smacks of being a Jew? And as if that*

wasn't bad enough, my sister-in-law Perl was a strictly religious woman who couldn't put up with her husband's shenanigans. She took to bed for days on end, she cried such buckets over her fate that it actually made her ill. At first it was nothing serious, then it got worse and worse—until one day, I'm sorry to say, poor Perl passed away.[9]

The description parallels any modern description of addictive behavior. The man's gambling addiction ultimately led to his and his family's demise, as do similar addictions today. Clearly, addiction was not absent among Jews. They knew what the toxic behavior patterns looked like, and they and their families suffered the consequences. *Still*, you might argue, *addiction might have been rare in Eastern Europe.* The fact that there were addicts among Jews doesn't tell us *how many* addicts there were. Maybe they were hard to come by?

Today, it seems likely that cases of Jewish addiction are rising. Because we keep things so hushed up, it is impossible to know. But the number of teen deaths, the number of Jewish addicts sitting in recovery meetings, and the number of people who simply reached out to contribute to this book testify that Jewish addiction is not as rare as we might have thought.

Judaism actually has many positive associations with alcohol and spirituality. There is a tradition associated with the "Shpoler Zeyde" (1725-1812) which states that "When a

---

[9]   Aleikhem, Sholom. Translation from Yiddish by Halkin, Hillel. *"It Doesn't Pay to be Good."* In: *"Tevye the Dairyman and the Railroad Stories."* Schocken, revised edition, 1996

man gives a cup of liquor to his friend to drink, it is true charity, for it seizes his heart and restores his spirit."[10] Likewise R' Nahman of Bratslav (1772-1810) taught that those who recite the ten psalms of the *tikkun ha-klali* (general rectification) are then "elevated by means of their drinking."[11] Even today, to create "happy" energy and to dispel depression and anxiety, or to wish the soul of a departed loved one an elevation in the afterlife ("The neshama should have an aliyah!"), drinking is encouraged.

Assimilation and Exposure to Mass Media

Outside of the uniquely Jewish sources of increased alcohol use, it is impossible to ignore the unprecedented way that our community has been influenced by the culture around us. If it was once true that *shiker iz a goy*, it might have been because Jews led profoundly different lives from the Gentiles surrounding them.

Dr. Glenn Dynner, an authority on Eastern European Jewry, writes that while Jews were heavily involved with the Gentiles in their midst, interacting primarily in matters of business, it would be a mistake to call them *integrated*. He draws on the writing of Antony Polonsky, who wrote that "the two groups lived in a hostile, but symbiotic relationship, marked both by a degree of social distance, which was lined with mutual disdain, and by strong economic links."[12]

---

[10]   Abraham ben Yehiel, *Hesed le-Avraham* (Czernowitz, 1884), introduction by Yehiel Shapiro of Tomaszil, n.p.

[11]   Nahman of Bratslav, *Likute etzot* (Lwow, 1858), "Brit," no. 29

[12]   *The Jews in Poland and Russia, Volume II: 1881-1914* (Oxford: Littman Library of Jewish Civilization, 2010), two volumes, 196

Yet as Jews made their way across the ocean, integration with Gentile society became more common. By the 1920s, the *allright-niks*—the Jews who had begun to make a decent living for themselves—were able to move out of tenement neighborhoods like the Lower East Side and find homes for themselves in formerly all-Gentile suburbs. What happens when we join a social milieu? Frequently, we imitate it.

So perhaps these Jews began to do what their neighbors did, which included using (and abusing) alcohol more often. It is no secret that Jews in America have moved away from Orthodoxy, with its teachings of restraint around alcohol. In the process, they may have found it was okay to drink like everybody else.

But American assimilation has gone further than geographic closeness. Yes, leaving the shtetl opens the door to outside influence. But external influence has a way of getting into our homes even when our homes remain in predominantly Jewish neighborhoods. This is through mass media.

As we introduce TVs and computers into the home, so do we introduce an advertising culture that makes alcohol look like an acceptable way to celebrate one's happy events and drown one's sorrows. What's a sporting event on TV without beer ads—or today, ads for hard liquor? Even if you don't have a TV in your home or use the internet, billboards celebrating all forms of alcohol abound along our highways. As we've noted, college life for decades has centered on the use and abuse of alcohol. On weekends, assimilated Jews go to bars just as did their Gentile friends and neighbors. Jews have a chameleon-like ability to assume the protective coloration of the surrounding community. It's part of our survival mechanism. And since Americans drank, perhaps so, in increasing numbers, did Jews.

Yet despite what seems to be a gradual shift in our community toward rising addiction, we still believe, as we did in the Old Country, that *shiker iz a goy*. Today, there is even a genetic explanation for why Jews aren't alcoholics. According to one study, 20 percent of Jews have the ADH2*2 gene, which makes alcohol easier to metabolize, and also creates more unpleasant reactions to alcohol[13]. Even if this is true, this slice of genetics offers no protection from alcoholism to the 80 percent or so of Jews who lack it. As for other forms of addiction—it offers no protection at all.

Jewish Life Is Stressful!

Another factor that may be contributing to the rising use of alcohol and other substances, especially in the Orthodox world, is our increasing levels of stress. One way an addiction is formed is as a treatment for emotional pain. It serves to reason, then, that added emotional pain in our lives might make us more likely to turn to the bottle, needle, or elsewhere.

It's no secret that modern life is stressful. People today, who might have once run a simple shop or trade, now juggle several jobs, travel long commutes, and spend excessive time sitting without a diet or exercise to balance these ill effects. Not surprisingly, stress levels are on the rise. Might addiction rise with it?

---

[13] Neumark YD, Friedlander Y, Thomasson HR, Li TK. Association of the ADH2*2 allele with reduced ethanol consumption in Jewish men in Israel: a pilot study. J Stud Alcohol. 1998 Mar;59(2):133-9. doi: 10.15288/jsa.1998.59.133. PMID: 9500299.

Stress in the Orthodox community has its own unique (and very strong!) flavor. We tend to have big families in the Orthodox community. It's not uncommon to see Orthodox families with six, eight, or even more children. Kids are expensive under any circumstances, but when you're paying the so-called "Orthodox tax," the financial pressure is all but unbearable.

What's the Orthodox tax? Day school tuition, not free public school. Renting or buying a home in an Orthodox neighborhood, so that you can walk to synagogue. This means living in homes that are inevitably more expensive than similar homes in non-Orthodox areas. The expectation of synagogue membership, *tzedakah* or charitable giving, and the higher cost of kosher food (including the considerably higher cost of kosher meat).

There's also the high cost of accouterments like tefillin for the men or wigs for the ladies, religious texts that must be purchased for oneself and one's children, and the spending seems to be endless in the run-up to Passover. Whatever it costs to raise a child in secular America, you can multiply that figure by, say, 70 percent, and you begin to approach the true cost of living for Orthodox families.

When our children were born, my mother used to quote the Yiddish expression that roughly translates as "Children bring their own mazel," meaning that if God gives you the child, God also gives you the means to support the child. That expression works better, alas, in theory than in practice, especially in situations where the father learns all day and the mom somehow has the responsibility not just to feed, clothe, bathe, and organize the lives of a large number of small children, but also has to find the money to pay for their needs.

You might say, "Yeah, but having children is stabilizing. How many parent addicts do you know?" There are more than you might think. Having a child is hardly a bar to addiction or alcoholism. The woman whose ex-husband I mentioned earlier, who died of a drug overdose, had been in recovery. When did he first start to relapse, you ask? After the birth of his first child.

That may seem surprising, but if you consider the challenges that accompany parenthood, it shouldn't be. For many, the *idea* of raising a family is exciting and meaningful. The *reality* of it, with all of its concomitant stresses, is enough to bring any already fragile person to a breaking point.

In fact, having a child is essentially pouring Miracle-Gro on whatever internal struggles addicts and alcoholics may already be experiencing. Add the challenges of sleeplessness, distraction, mess, noise, and ballooning costs. Having a young child or a few young children makes it considerably more difficult to attend twelve-step meetings…while increasing the occasional feeling of needing to escape. The addict all too often goes back to his or her drug of choice. Fortunately, twelve-step meetings via Zoom, prevalent since the onset of the COVID pandemic, make it considerably easier for parents to tap into recovery without leaving the house. But kids, despite the fact that they are the greatest blessing to which one could aspire, complicate everything—marriage, money, and sobriety.

The financial burden of raising an Orthodox family is likewise not for the faint of heart. Couples who have invested their efforts in Torah study, with less of a focus on earning a living, may not have started a career sufficient to support a family. As a result, family stress quickly compounds. We're not allowed to talk about that stress, of course. It would look like we are complaining about Hashem's will for us. But let's not kid ourselves. The toll of raising large families under such conditions is enormous. Stress needs relief. Relief is at hand on Friday nights and Shabbat mornings, and any time a drink, a pill, or a gambling app, can be found. Which is 24/7/365.

Rabbi Nahum Simon, Ph.D., has devoted his career to helping Jewish addicts in recovery. Rabbi Simon suggests another possible cause for rising addiction in the Jewish community. He states that the psychological displacement of coming from a familiar, comfortable world into a world where one has no bearings—as did Eastern European Jews prior to and after World War II—may easily have contributed to a rise in addiction:

> The male immigrant was faced with feelings of displacement in the new country. This applies mainly to the male head of household, struggling to speak a new language, dealing with a foreign culture and, frequently, the inability to find employment. The feelings became unbearable and solace was sought in alcohol. The proud man did not want to rely on his children for assistance. In those years, it never occurred to us to consider that the problem was one of alcoholism rather than a societal issue.
>
> The fact is that there is no reason to believe that Jews differ from the general population in the occurrence of alcoholism and addiction. The percentage of Jews participating in

recovery programs or seeking treatment will generally parallel the percentage of Jews living among the general population.[14]

Here, Simon suggests that we may have been mistaken in our assumptions about Jewish sobriety all along. To the extent that alcoholism is a disease, why should it be less prevalent among Jews, after all? Whether this has always been the case, or whether addiction has gradually gone up in the Jewish community, it is hard to say. That we must face the issue head-on, however, we know.

A Post-Traumatic Stress Generation

Once we are speaking about the potential for stress to encourage addictive behavior, it becomes impossible to avoid another trauma affecting Jews today—and one with which I, like millions of other Jews, have a strong personal connection. Of course, I'm talking about the Holocaust.

For many young people in their teens to their thirties, the Holocaust has a different meaning than it does for people of my generation (I was born in 1958, thirteen years after World War II ended). For the younger generation, the Holocaust is a metaphor for evil, an exercise in understanding the worst in human nature. It may be a source of horror and brutal shock to contemplate, but something mercifully receding in history, like the American Civil War.

---

[14]   Simon, Nahum. *"Alcoholism and the Jewish Community."* Seaside Palm Beach Premier Addiction Treatment Center, https://www.seasidepalm-beach.com/addiction-blog/alcoholism-and-jewish-community/

For families like mine—who knew the people who were murdered or who somehow escaped—the Holocaust still remains a large, gaping, inexplicable, and emotionally unmanageable hole in the soul. It's something we think about, if not every day, then almost every day. For us, the Holocaust is not a metaphor. It is a living, breathing entity that forces us to ask over and over and over, why them, and why not us? It forces the children and grandchildren of survivors (my mother escaped Europe by the skin of her teeth when she was four years old) to live with an imaginary yellow star pinned to our clothing that says, in despicable German block print, *Jude.*

Not long ago, my wife and I went out to dinner with friends on a freezing January night. My friend wasn't wearing a winter coat, and I asked her why not. She explained that years ago she had read Primo Levi's account of his experiences in concentration camps and how cold he was all the time. She deliberately chose not to wear winter coats, even on freezing nights, as a tribute to Jews who had suffered through the freezing cold in the camps. It brought to mind William Faulkner's line, "The past is never dead. It's not even past." On the one hand, it's a noble gesture. On the other hand, retelling the story essentially retraumatizes the listener. It indicated the level of trauma that my friend still endures. So many of us are that way. We're all walking around in the dead of winter without our coats on.

More recently, I went with a friend my age to a matzah-baking event prior to Passover at a Jewish school in Riverdale, New York. After we rolled and flattened the dough, we watched as the baker took the pieces of unleavened bread and fired them for twenty seconds in an oven heated, we were told, to 1,200 degrees Fahrenheit. As we gazed at the oven, my friend said, "My daughter's in Poland. Her school group visited Auschwitz yesterday." Okay, tell me what other group on Earth looks at ovens and thinks about the things we Jews think about.

The after-effects of the Holocaust haunt our waking thoughts, hold us hostage to survivor guilt, and triggers nightmares when we sleep. It affects numbers of children we have and the names we give those children. Then, when we name children after our relatives, those who survived and those who didn't, we feel guilty for burdening our children with the trauma that burdens us.

The Shoah ended almost eighty years ago, but the psychological turmoil it created in our community is still present. Untreated Holocaust trauma doesn't just vanish; it is passed from parent to child and becomes part of our spiritual DNA. The father who is emotionally withdrawn, the mother who lashes out because she bears the anger that her parents did not feel permission to feel, may well raise children so immersed in emotional pain that addiction may easily become the solution, and, dare I say it, all too often the final solution.

People who do not connect to the pain of the Holocaust personally may find this difficult to believe. But for those of us who grew up with the consciousness of mass human suffering in the background of our lives, it is not an impossible stretch. My mother told me that my grandmother received a postcard—a *postcard*!—from the Red Cross, informing her that her six brothers had been shot to death at the family lumberyard in Poland. She cried for a day and then never brought it up again. How did I feel when I heard this? How did I feel about my own existence and survival, next to their brutal murders? Human beings are not equipped to process such evil, nor to carry the burden of such emotional pain. Trauma needs something to smooth it over, and here comes alcohol or substance use to do just that.

And it's not just the Holocaust. It's centuries of murder, rape, forced conscription, exile, convert or die, pogroms, Cossacks, what have you. This is who we are. This is as much a part of Jewish identity, like it or not, admit it or not, as winning outsized numbers of Nobel Prizes, comedians from the Marx Brothers to Jackie Mason, bagels and lox, and Yiddishisms embedded in the English language. It's in us. It *is* us.

Cognitive Dissonance

Though the issue of the Holocaust affects Jews of all denominations, I believe it's harder if you're Orthodox. This is because you can't shove the *tzadik v'ra lo* question—the issue of how bad things can happen to innocent, righteous people—under some imaginary rug. That's because if you're an observant Jew, you must organize your life around prayer and service to God. You have to pray at least three times a day, which means that you're either asking God three times a day how He could have committed the Shoah, how he could have stood idly by, or whether He wanted it, or what, if anything, it all means. Otherwise, you're sticking your ancestral memory of the Holocaust in your proverbial back pocket so that you can pray to a God who allows such things to happen.

You have to struggle with the question of how you can call God good, or the source of good, or the protector, or the savior, as our prayers insist when you know full well that for those six horrible years, He allowed such unspeakable evil to flourish. And so, added to the emotional pain of the Holocaust is the cognitive dissonance that continued faith forces on it. Given that the solution to addiction involves turning to God, it is not surprising that the pain and confusion that pushes us away from Him might well become a pathway to addiction in the first place.

***

It is impossible to know for certain what our people's past and present relationship to alcoholism has been. Was early Jewish sobriety exaggerated? Have we always been as likely to be drunks as everyone else? Or has addiction crept up on us slowly, due to the forces of assimilation, Holocaust trauma, or some other hidden causes? Answers to these questions are beyond the scope of my limited experience and knowledge base. But we do know that thousands of Jews are suffering under the burden of addiction today, and they need us to leave behind our outdated notion that *shiker iz a goy* if we want to help them along the path to recovery.

Wherever it came from, addiction is here in the Jewish community. And it appears to be here to stay.

CHAPTER 4

Addiction and Orthodoxy: The State of Play

B efore we begin to consider how to address the problem of addiction in the overall Jewish community, we need to take a deeper dive into the manner in which addiction has affected the Orthodox world. Secular Jews may have the mixed blessing of overexposure to secular American culture. But they also have greater awareness of, comfort with, and access to forms of recovery from addiction and alcoholism, including twelve-step programs, therapy, medication, and other means. The Orthodox, less so, and thus we need to see what special challenges and concerns the Orthodox world faces.

No-Talk Rules

You might think that a community rooted in sacred traditions of loving one's fellow and compassion toward the needy might have a high degree of sensitivity to those in their midst whose life challenges have tipped them over from the casual use of unhealthy behaviors into addiction.

Alas, you would be wrong.

Psychologists speak of unhealthy "no-talk rules" that govern dysfunctional families. A "no-talk rule" is an unspoken rule by which a family member is not allowed to talk about what's happening in the family, no matter how bad it is, either with anyone inside the home or, God forbid, with anyone outside. Not surprisingly, you cannot have a healthy family and also have no-talk rules. Healthy families must be able to talk things out.

The Orthodox community, sad to say, seems to be governed by no-talk rules on a massive scale. When someone is struggling with a mental health issue, we don't like to talk about it. When someone is struggling with religion, we'd rather cover it up. When someone is struggling with addiction—does anyone know? And if they do, is there any alternative to silence?

In fact, many people across the Orthodox spectrum (YU, Charedi, Chabad, Sefardi, you name it) don't know what addiction is. They don't know what kind of help is needed or where it is available. They don't understand what recovery could look like. Why?? Why do we insist on keeping silent?? Why are we not trying to get help for people whose lives are literally at risk?

The Image of Perfection

To begin to answer this question, we need to do a little "Jewish psychoanalysis." When we do, we discover that Jewish self-esteem is built on some powerful beliefs. That God Himself spoke to us on Sinai. That our Torah is a complete and incomparable guide to life. That our people, as evidenced by the massive impact we have had throughout history despite our small numbers, are privileged, even superior in some way, due to our singular tradition, or genetics, or behaviors, or what-have-you.

So what happens when Jews slip up? Especially in the Orthodox community, where the above beliefs are central, how do we maintain our religious attitudes when we watch Jews failing to live up to the "Jewish standard," by suffering from an addiction?

Well, I can tell you how the Torah itself suggests that we relate to Jewish failure. There is inevitably charatah, kapparah, and teshuva—regret, atonement, return, and forgiveness. But let's first look at how the Orthodox *actually* relate to it. The mere thought of the existence of Jewish addicts makes us *ashamed*. Addiction is a *shonda*, and *shonda* must be avoided at all costs.

Now you might argue that secular Jews, or non-Jews, can experience shame, and it's just as painful for them. But let's look at what I mean by shame a little more closely. Yes, any person might feel *guilty* because we feel we've failed in some way. But guilt is practically built into the Jewish experience! That's not really our issue!

"Shame" describes how we feel when we know that *others are watching us* and seeing our mistakes. That feeling will always be more powerful within insular communities. A secular Jew, or a non-Jew, can do something that triggers shame—some sort of inappropriate behavior that the community finds out about. But then that person can move somewhere else and start a new life, where no one is the wiser.

Let me give you an example from my own life. When he was twelve, one of our sons took tennis lessons from an instructor in his late twenties who, according to news reports, sexually abused some of his other students while on overnight trips to tennis matches. We were incredibly lucky that this did not happen to our son. What happened to the perpetrator after we found out and pulled our son out of his classes? He left town.

He started over, as a tennis instructor, of course, in a small town in Texas. How do I know? Because after we parted ways, I looked him up on the internet. Did he ever go to prison? No. Did the people in his new community have the slightest idea of what he had done in his previous location? Doubtful. He was a sociopath, a molester, an abuser, and an individual with no regard for the humanity of others. Did he feel responsible for what he had done to the boys he had traumatized for life? Who knows? But did he feel shame because wherever he went, the story of what he had done would follow him? Of course not, because the story didn't follow him to his new community a thousand miles away.

If he had been a tennis instructor in the Orthodox world, however (if there were such a thing as an Orthodox tennis instructor), somebody from where he lived would know somebody from where he moved. The shame would follow him. It would attach to him like the mark of Cain.

The problem with acknowledging addiction in our midst is that to have a spouse or a child or a grandchild or a parent who is an alcoholic or addict of any stripe is an invitation to feel shame. It's an invitation to the community to close its eyes, shake its head, and say the worst word a Jew can pronounce about another Jew: shonda.

So why are we so ashamed when we face struggling members of our community? Well, it has to do with our Jewish psychoanalysis. For Orthodox Jews, our fellows' struggles don't just reflect on *them*, we feel they reflect on *us*—whether as parents, as teachers, or as a community. And some of the implications are not things we're willing to face.

How Can the Torah Not Solve All Our Problems?

First, the Orthodox believe the Torah is supposed to be entirely sufficient. It's God's blueprint for creating the world. Look into it and you can find the answer to any problem.

What happens to this belief when we discover addiction in our midst? First of all, we're forced to face the reality that religious life doesn't save us from falling prey to the effects of alcohol, heroin or gambling. Then, when we want to heal from addiction, we're forced to face the additional reality that there's no verse in the Torah that provides a direct solution for addiction. Now, pretty much everything in Alcoholics Anonymous is rooted in or similar to Torah concepts. The great authority on Judaism and recovery, Rabbi Abraham Twerski, once wrote that he would sue the founder of Alcoholics Anonymous for plagiarism because AA borrows so much from the Torah without giving credit. It's just that the revelation of the Torah and the creation of Alcoholics Anonymous happened about 3,500 years apart, and its founders weren't exactly Jewish. So even if the Twelve Steps match up with what the Torah teaches, it's hard to conclude that they *come* from the Torah. Yet the idea that we need to go beyond the Torah for something important just doesn't feel right. If it's not in the Torah, suggests this line of reasoning, then Jews don't need it. Unfortunately, this becomes strike one against recovery.

Whatever Happened to Jewish Superiority?

The next reason that acknowledging addiction is a source of shame for us is that it is a blemish on our sense of moral superiority. Whether or not you are comfortable admitting it, moral superiority pervades the Jewish identity. We've probably had it, say, since Sinai, when God pronounced us a "nation of priests" and "treasured among nations" (Ex. 19).

And since the time when shtetl Jews happily sang *shiker iz a goy*, the belief that Jews are not prone to addiction has fit quite comfortably into our superiority complex. So…a Jewish addict poses a challenge to that myth.

For one, we start to worry about our Jewish self-image. We like the idea of Jews as sober, levelheaded, and well-adjusted. When I was in yeshiva in Israel in the early 1980s, one of my buddies from Staten Island, which had large non-Jewish and Orthodox Jewish populations, told me that Gentile mothers were delighted when their daughters married Jewish men. "They're happy," he told me, "because they know their husbands aren't going to get drunk and beat up their wives or spend the paycheck on booze and women before they get home."

Now, if you're Jewish, you probably love hearing this story. It not only reaffirms a sense of Jewish protection against the evils of secular society and substance abuse, but it provides evidence of a phenomenon we are all secretly looking out for—that non-Jews recognize how prized our culture and habits are as well. Not surprisingly, the discovery that some Jewish men *do* spend their paycheck on alcohol, and in some cases, *do* come down on their wives is highly unsettling for us. We think that we're better than that. Don't tell us otherwise!

Perhaps more importantly, don't let the news slip to those Gentile mothers that their stereotype of Jewish men is not universally upheld. No, no, we cannot let other people know that we suffer from the same human failings that they do. By acknowledging alcoholism and addiction in our midst, we are testifying negatively against ourselves, and we are admitting that we aren't supermen and superwomen. Better not to say anything. Let's just pretend that this isn't our problem. Shh. The *goyim* are listening.

The Narrowing of the "Path"

Okay, so let's stop for a minute and go back to our first question: What do the Orthodox supposedly believe they are *supposed to do* when they confront moral challenges and failures within their community? Rather than turning inward to face our challenges and working to help the Jews who are struggling among us, we've done the opposite. We've turned outward to try to project a perfect image of our community while hushing up anything inside that might not match that image.

Today, Orthodoxy offers less of a *derech* or specific path and more of a *tayvah*, or Ark. The Ark was built to preserve a small sample of humanity, as well as representative couples from the animal kingdom, at a time of unspeakable evil. Only a few, Noah and his seven relatives, survived. Orthodoxy today is a tayvah of sorts from which its inhabitants peer down onto a sea of assimilation and rejection.

Noah's reputation is a mixed bag. On the one hand, he was a tsaddik who walked with God. On the other hand, he did not do enough to cause his generation to repent, even though he had more than a century to work on it. The tayvah or Ark was completed, filled, and launched. The rains began, and all those not on board drowned. And the ship sailed serenely on.

All too often today, that's us.

Chabad and some other groups make a practice of "in-reach," trying to be *m'karev* (to bring back to religion) Jews who either slipped off the derech or have never heard of the derech. The rest of us are complicit in sailing on a modern-day Noah's Ark. We aren't even looking over the side of the boat to see whether someone is waiting for us to toss them a lifeline. Instead, we're shrugging and saying, "What do you expect? They aren't frum enough." Maybe we, too, walk with God. But we're no better than Noah when it comes to our fellow man.

Cast Outside the Camp

How does this affect the way that we deal with addicts in our community? I want to share with you what the model for treatment of alcoholics and addicts in our community appears to be. When Jews were in the desert after they left Egypt, and before they circumnavigated their way into the Promised Land, the most common affliction described in the pages of the Bible was something called *tzaraat* (Lev. 13).

The simplest, although somewhat inaccurate, translation of *tzaraat* is leprosy. More accurately, tzaraat was a skin disease that afflicted Jews, not just in the midbar but also when the Jews entered the Promised Land. The Talmud goes to great lengths to describe different kinds of tzaraat, including their color, size, location on the body, and what to do about it.

In fact, our tradition understands tzaraat as a function of *lashon hara*, which roughly translates as evil speech or gossip. Most famously, when Miriam, the sister of Moses, spoke disparagingly of him, she was struck with tzaraat on her arm (Num. 12:10). In short, tzaraat was a medical issue that represented a spiritual transgression in the person struck with the disease.

What was the "treatment" for tzaraat? According to Torah law, it was to put the sufferers outside the camp for a period and then, under certain circumstances, readmit them. What did it mean to be placed outside the camp? Was it temporary ex-communication? Was it a punishment? Or was it a means of isolating a person from contaminating his tribe, either physically or spiritually? Probably all the above.

Fast forward to our times. In place of tzaraat, we have different physical manifestations of a spiritual illness: drug and alcohol addiction. What do we do with the sufferers? It seems like we do the same thing we did with them back in the times of the desert. We shove them outside the camp. In some cases, we ignore their existence. In others, we quite literally cast them out.

In Brooklyn, Monsey, and Lakewood, among other Orthodox strongholds, some families valiantly seek treatment for their loved ones. Many others, unfortunately, simply put those kids on planes to Los Angeles, where the addicted young people become the problem to solve for Chabad, Beit T'Shuvah, or any other institution trying to create the possibility of recovery for Jewish addicts and alcoholics. Whether it's outside the camp in the desert or outside the community and off to the rehabs of Southern California, the problem and solution haven't changed in thousands of years.

Get rid of the person.

Don't talk about it.

Move on.

Are We Throwing Our Addicts Away?

But the laws governing tzaraat are God-given and meant to apply to a specific case. In general, Jews have a mitzvah to care for the sick and to raise up those who have fallen down—not to ostracize them.

A recovering alcoholic once told about how he had driven his car, with his brother in the backseat, into the town junkyard while in an alcoholic blackout. When they woke up and realized the nature of their surroundings, one said to the other, "They threw us away!"

Obviously, this alcoholic hadn't literally been thrown into the junkyard by his family and community. He had driven himself there. But the Jewish approach has always been to take responsibility for one another and to step in when our brother is in trouble. *Lo ta'amod al dam rei'echa*—Do not stand idly by the blood of your fellow (Lev. 19:16)—famously obligates us to step in when another Jew is being harmed. "Whoever is able to save [a person] and does not save violates this commandment!" says the Rambam.[15] If that's the

---

[15]   Mishneh Torah, Laws of the Murderer and Protecting Life

case, then when addicts fall off the map, don't we bear some of the blame? Do we really want to throw away our children and grandchildren, our spouses and parents, just because they're struggling? We have no right to leave them stranded.

Can We Get Our Priorities Straight?

Narrowing the derech and protecting the image of communal perfection, though done in the name of a higher level of observance, is compromising our true observance of Judaism. While we may perform more rituals, study more ancient texts, and earn more "mitzvah points," what is all of this worth if we are neglecting our responsibilities *bein adam le'chavero*—between man and his friend?

Perhaps this is why on Yom Kippur, we read the passage in Isaiah 58, in which we are told,

> *Is such the fast that I have chosen? The day for*
> *a man to afflict his soul?*
> *Is it to bow down his head as a bulrush, And to*
> *spread sackcloth and ashes under him?*
> *Wilt thou call this a fast, And an acceptable*
> *day to the LORD?*
>
> *Is not this the fast that I have chosen? To loose*
> *the fetters of wickedness,*
> *To undo the bands of the yoke, And to let the*
> *oppressed go free,*
> *And that ye break every yoke?*

Is it not to deal thy bread to the hungry,
And that thou bring the poor that are cast out
to thy house?
When thou seest the naked, that thou
cover him,
And that thou hide not thyself from thine own
flesh?[16]

It's true that addiction creates unique challenges in a person's life. And it's true that we don't want to enable addicts to buy more booze, drugs, or tokens for the slot machines. But addicts are usually individuals who are struggling deeply and who need acceptance and support.

But because we Orthodox live by what the Mafia calls a code of *omertá*, enforced silence, we've made it all but impossible for addiction to speak its name and for families who are affected to seek help. How many individuals would be able to seek treatment if they knew that they and their families would not be stigmatized for having done so? How many families would be spared the trauma of separation and divorce if knowledge of Al-Anon, the support group for families of addicts, was commonplace? How many Jews would still find a home in Judaism, despite the fact that their paths weren't quite up to an impossibly high standard?

When Self-Sufficiency Becomes Self-Destruction

While we touch on the ways that addiction challenges our Orthodox self-image, I have to mention one more factor:

---

[16]   Isaiah 58:5-7

Orthodox people believe strongly that we should not out-source our problems but that we are fully capable of "han-dling our business" from the inside.

In Europe, perhaps the worst thing you could call a fel-low Jew was a *moser*, an informer, one who ratted on his fel-low Jew to the secular authorities, who were only too happy to punish the person singled out. In Eastern European com-munities, the punishment for being a moser was often death.

Today, we no longer call informants moserim. But the same ethos prevails—if there's a problem, we are going to handle it internally. We can send you to this rav, or that rab-binical court, and we can get the matter handled ourselves without any external help.

Now, self-sufficiency is generally a good thing. It's great that we want to handle our problems internally. The ques-tion is whether we *can*. Today, the Orthodox community still has only a relatively small number of organized resources for helping individuals afflicted with addiction or alcoholism. So here we have quite the double-bind. We can only look to our community to help, but our community is all but incapable of providing help.

We need to lay aside our pride and seek help to save the lives of the many Jews who are struggling with life-threaten-ing addictions. And when the community has evolved to the point that it can be self-sufficient in dealing with addiction, we can throw a big recovery party together!

The Costs of Casting Aside

It's common knowledge among addicts in recovery that as an addict, there are three places you can end up: in recovery, in prison, or in the cemetery. It might take a little while, but eventually, it is always one of those three.

As an example, did you know that approximately 100,000 Americans died in 2021 from drug overdoses?[17] That's practically twice the number of all Americans killed during the Vietnam War. If you've ever been to the Vietnam War Memorial in Washington DC, imagine a wall twice as high with twice as many names. And that would just cover the deaths from just one calendar year.

By closing our community off from acknowledging our struggles, by prioritizing our image over our individuals, by narrowing the "path" and making it harder and harder for Jews to stay within the community, we are setting our brothers up so that their names will appear, sooner than later, on the memorial wall for drug and alcohol abusers.

It's time to change. We need to be sending rowboats to rescue those who need help, those who have fallen off of the Ark into the icy waters below. But before we can do that, we have to acknowledge that even we Orthodox Jews are not immune to addiction and alcoholism. We are taught to regard one life as having the value of an entire world. Each Jewish addict needs help, and it's time we started facing reality and saving worlds, one at a time.

---

[17] Centers for Disease Control and Prevention, (2021, Nov. 17) "*Drug Overdose Deaths in the U.S. Top 100,000 Annually.*" https://www.cdc.gov/nchs/pressroom/nchs_press_releases/2021/20211117.htm

CHAPTER 5

Where Does Addiction Come From, Anyway?

W hy do we stigmatize things? Usually, it's because we don't understand them. We are afraid of the unknown, and we look down on things that we can't comprehend. One thing that most people can't comprehend is people destroying their health, ruining their relationships, and spending all their money on an addictive substance or behavior. When we meet that, we start pointing fingers. *What kind of terrible person does these things? Why won't he pull it together and just quit? Does she think we don't realize what she's doing behind our backs?*

Addicts can do some pretty terrible things. And they should and will be held responsible for those things. But the attitude of blaming an addict doesn't entirely make sense—because, by definition, once someone is struggling with an addiction, she has lost control of herself. In truth, if we want to shift our mindset from shame and blame toward addicts to support and healing, the first step is understanding what addiction is and why it happens.

When Addiction Is Purely Physical

It is known that a person can become physically dependent on a substance and even, to some extent, a behavior when they use it regularly. The body naturally adapts to regular exposure to the substance, such that when it is taken away, even if it was originally prescribed by a doctor, the person experiences withdrawal symptoms while the body readjusts to not having the substance.[18]

Typically, the addict or alcoholic will crave the substance to relieve the withdrawal symptoms. In this way, even an otherwise healthy person can develop an addiction simply by using a substance regularly enough. Once a person reaches this point of dependency, he starts to seek the substance compulsively, despite its negative consequences. The compulsion to use is so strong that few people have the power to resist.

Even for addicts who didn't end up addicts because of using highly addictive substances, every addiction eventually becomes a physical addiction. The reward center in the brain starts to *expect* the relief that you get from using, whether that relief is chemical or psychological, and it becomes harder and harder to resist the physical craving.

---

[18] National Institute on Drug Abuse, *"The Science of Drug Use and Addiction: The Basics"* (2018, July 2). Media Guide. https://archives.drugabuse.gov/publications/media-guide/science-drug-use-addiction-basics

At the same time, the more a person uses, the more his body habituates to the substance and the more of his substance of choice he needs in order to get his "fix." Recovering drug addicts will tell you about the challenge of chasing the high—that original sense of release they felt, once upon a time, with their drugs. I once asked a friend why she smoked, when she knew how bad it was for her. Her answer was fascinating to me: "I smoke because every time I light up, it reminds me of the first time I ever smoked." In other words, it's all about chasing a long-lost, and often never-to-return, high.

Escape from Pain

Perhaps a more common reason that people become addicts is because they are trying to escape pain. Here's the definition I would use: *Addiction is unhealthy behavior meant to kill emotional pain.*

But isn't pain a part of life? you might ask. We all experience pain. We say as much in *Pirkei Avot*, advice meant for all of us:

> *Against your will were you formed, against your will were you born, against your will you live, against your will you will die, and against your will you will give an account and reckoning before the King of the kings of kings, the Holy One, blessed be He. (Avot 4:22)*

Nothing along the way is easy. Being born isn't easy, teething isn't easy, emotional pain of childhood isn't easy, dealing with being teased or bullied isn't easy, feeling insecure isn't easy, growing up isn't easy, getting educated isn't easy, finding the right spouse or partner isn't easy, raising kids isn't easy, making a living isn't easy, getting older isn't easy, and often dying isn't easy. There's pain in practically every phase of life, but that's just how the world was created. The same *Pirke Avot* also educates us that *le'fum tzara agra*—According to the pain is the reward (Ibid. 5:23).

Pain is not inherently bad but can actually be good and a productive part of living. But there's a wonderful expression in the recovery community, which has a knack for reducing home truths to snappy phrases: *Pain is mandatory, suffering is optional.* Pain is a part of life, no matter what. But whether that pain causes us to suffer is not. Suffering is optional, or, in some cases—if we didn't choose it—it is still unnecessary.

So, where does suffering come from? Sometimes we suffer because we haven't treated our pain. If you've got a toothache and you fail to go to the dentist, you'll go from pain to suffering pretty darn quickly. The same can be true with emotional pain. If you don't treat it, it turns into suffering, and eventually, it becomes unbearable. Feelings are like TNT—the more tightly they're packed, the bigger the explosion later on.

There are healthy ways to treat emotional pain. But what happens when you don't *know* those ways? What happens when because of who you are or the environment you are in, you become trapped in your emotional pain and have no way to climb out? This is where addiction comes in. Imagine living with a toothache and being nowhere near a dentist. The toothache gets worse and worse until the pain is throbbing throughout your head and body. You can't think. You can't eat. You can't *exist*. All you can focus on is finding a way to get away from the horrible pain.

Then you discover that when you get drunk, the pain is dulled. Or when you use narcotics. Or distract yourself with gambling or another fix. Would you continue to go back to that behavior, to escape the unbearable pain that you're living with? You just might, even though you know it's morally wrong and can lead to many bad outcomes. You just want to get out of the pain, so you ignore all the consequences. In fact, one of the myriad expressions for getting drunk is "feeling no pain"—and that's exactly the point. *People get drunk because it takes them out of the present moment.*

The present moment is the "place" where we experience pain, whether it's a loss or resentment relating to the past or a fear relating to something that may or may not happen in the future. Acting out through an addiction offers temporary relief from the emotional pain we were sitting in a moment before.

Now, there's nothing wrong *per se* with alcohol or even with enjoying the uplifting effects of having a small drink. We might have a little schnapps at a *yahrzeit*, a service where we acknowledge the anniversary of the passing of a loved one. We say, "The *neshama* should have an *aliyah*," meaning that the soul of the departed should rise another level in heaven. And with that nip of Scotch, our spirits do rise. That's why they call booze spirits! But the question is whether the booze is giving us spirit to engage in our lives, or we're using the spirits to run away.

Once we get the essence of addiction, it's easy to see how any behavior can be weaponized into an addictive pattern that has a temporary benefit of killing pain but a long-term drawback of killing us. There are people who spend four hours a day in the gym exercising. Trust me, most of these people are not going to the Olympics. And they're not extending their lifespans, either. Instead, they are using exercise as a way of avoiding pain, just as the alcoholic uses alcohol or the drug addict uses marijuana or cocaine.

You can eat too much, you can eat too little; you can spend yourself into massive credit card debt, enjoying the temporary thrill of purchasing something, only to fall victim to massive remorse when the credit card bill comes through. You can work yourself into an early grave or simply work so hard that you can justify avoiding contact with loved ones because "work comes first." Booze. Drugs. Gambling. Overeating. Starving ourselves. Spending too much. Being miserly. What do all these things have in common?

They are behaviors that keep us out of the present moment because that's where the pain can be found. So if you've ever asked yourself, "Why does that person drink so much?!" or "Why does he run up so much credit card debt?" or "Why can't he go one Sunday without betting hundreds on the Jets[19]?" or "Doesn't she realize that her behavior can come with a huge price?" the answer's always the same: *They're doing it to kill pain. The other consequences are far too distant to imagine.*

Where Is This Pain Coming From?

When we define addiction as a way of trying to treat emotional pain, the natural question is—where is all this pain

---

[19] If you're a Jets fan, this book won't help you. Nothing can.

coming from? We know that life is painful for everyone, but why do addicts have so *much* pain, or why do they have so much difficulty *treating it?*

Pain of Trauma

One possible source of emotional pain is childhood or adolescent trauma. And we could be talking severe trauma—like physical or sexual abuse—or relatively minor sources of trauma that may not seem so severe on the surface but can eat away at a person from the inside.

When I was growing up, I remember that adults in our family would look at me as if they had some sort of horrible, unspeakable news to deliver, but I was just too young to hear it. My parents fled the Holocaust, but many of their family members did not make it. The sense of a hovering, inexplicable injustice pervaded our lives. And there were unspoken boundaries everywhere—things we couldn't talk about, couldn't ask about—because they were too painful. Growing up around people with a lot of untreated pain kind of presents a double-whammy. It passes the pain on to you while giving you no tools for dealing with it or even a framework for understanding what that pain is all about.

Of course, it goes without saying that more acute trauma—like experiencing abandonment, physical abuse, sexual abuse, or the loss of important family members—can also drive a person to the point that addiction becomes the solution. But linking addiction to trauma isn't fair all the time, especially for loving, healthy, non-addicted parents whose children inexplicably become addicts. Parenting is hard, and we have enough things to beat ourselves up about without wondering whether we caused our kid to turn to addiction (spoiler alert: you didn't).

Pain of the Broken Self

Sometimes, we can't find a source or a starting point for an addict's pain. Sometimes the person grew up well, came from a happy home, and should have "no reason" to turn to booze or drugs. And yet they do, and not just because the substance is physically addictive, but because they are trying to run away from their pain. What is this pain??

Rabbi Y.Y. Jacobson says that an addict's pain is the pain of *feeling oneself too much.* Have you ever heard the expression "being uncomfortable in your skin?" Some people feel that just being present and aware is painful because it means being connected to their sense of *self.*

For whatever reason, some of us feel this way, that we constantly need to get out of our*selves.* We're so disgusted by what we see, or we feel so inadequate about who we are, that being in touch is just unbearably painful. Better to numb my sense of self so I don't have to feel it anymore. Better to turn my brain off and start drinking, or using, or shopping, or betting compulsively, so I don't have to remember how terrible it feels to be alive.

There's a great metaphor for this. If you think about the body, it is most healthy when you don't notice it. When nothing is hurting, when you're not tired or aching, when your body is just doing what it needs to do—that is a body at its healthiest. When parts of it start to hurt, we become conscious of those parts. We suddenly notice the back that is aching or the finger that is burning or the head that is throbbing.

The same is true with the self. A healthy sense of self is one that is not felt too strongly. The more we start to *notice* ourselves, the more uncomfortable we become. Or to flip it around—the more injured our sense of self, the more conscious of it we become. An addict is usually someone who can't notice himself because, like an aching back, his sense of self is constantly hurting him.

If you lived with a roommate who was constantly insulting, hurting, and harassing you, you would try to get away from that roommate, right? The addict has that roommate in his head. It is his own inner voice, and living with it on a constant basis becomes a form of torture. The only solution is escaping to a state where he doesn't have to feel it anymore!

Understanding this should help us stop judging addicts who appear to come from healthy families and have no apparent basis for their addiction. We cannot judge another person until we have walked a mile in their shoes. We don't know what subtle psychological forces may be at play that are causing the person to use. But we can usually assume that if a person is using, he or she is not all that happy about it and may feel a deep sense of inner brokenness.

When meeting with an addict or alcoholic, therefore, I propose that we approach with caution and with compassion. Usually, there are deep wounds underneath the shooting up or the booze-guzzling. Understanding this is the first step in being able to help.

CHAPTER 6

The Disease and its Cure

One of the recovered alcoholics I spoke with for this book shared something that someone told him about addiction. The first Step in Alcoholics Anonymous is "We admitted we were powerless over alcohol—that our lives had become unmanageable."

He said, "I never understood this until another alcoholic explained it like this: You're driving on a road and you come to a fork in the road. You stop and decide which way to go. You go left. The next time you're driving down that same road, you go left again. You keep going left until, at some point, you stop seeing the fork entirely. It's as if it isn't there. You're going to go left no matter what happens.

"That's the way I became with drinking," he explained. "At some point, I stopped thinking about whether to drive to the bar after work to get smashed. I just did it. Again and again until I couldn't choose not to. I had become powerless over alcohol."

Willpower Doesn't Help

Normies (people who aren't addicts) tend to look at addicts and wonder why they can't just "Say no to drugs!" or "Say no to alcohol!" or other forms of addictive behavior. What they don't understand is that the choice of saying "no" left that addict a long time ago. And when addicts think they can beat their addiction through sheer force of will—the result is usually a series of false starts that end in ultimate relapse. This is why willpower has little relevance in the life of the addict or the lifecycle of an addiction. Willpower implies that you can make a choice. Addicts can't make choices; their addictions make their choices for them. They know, in some dim, dark corner of their mind, that this isn't going to end well. Maybe they'll get away with it this time, but ultimately, they know they're doomed. They know they're never going to get this right, and they know that even if they can stop themselves for a short while, it's only a matter of time until they go right back to their drug of choice.

I've seen heroin addicts in treatment centers who have spiderweb tattoos on their faces because that's how they see themselves. A fly caught in a spiderweb. I've never seen a more accurate or chilling physical rendering of what addiction looks or feels like. Now, you might say, "But don't Jews believe in free choice? How can you say that willpower stops working!?" Well, you might be surprised to discover what Judaism *actually* says about free choice.

Here is a quote from the Talmud, tractate Kiddushin, page 30b:

> *And Rabbi Shimon ben Levi says: A person's inclination overpowers him every day, and seeks to kill him, as it is stated: "The wicked watches the righteous and seeks to slay him" (Psalms 37:32).* **And if not for the fact that the Holy One, Blessed be He, assists each person in battling his evil inclination, he could not overcome it,** *as it is stated: "The Lord will not leave him in his hand" (Psalms 37:33).*

Yes, Judaism might believe in free choice, but even Jews look at free choice as a God-given or God-assisted process. According to the Talmud, without God's help, no one would "overcome their evil inclination." So are you really so surprised that addicts, who usually leave God out of the picture while they sell themselves out to a substance, have trouble overcoming their addiction?

Here's another Jewish attitude about wrongdoing, also from the Talmud, tractate Sotah, page 3a:

> *Raish Lakish says: A man does not commit a transgression unless a spirit of insanity enters into him.*

If insanity is the source of transgression, does it make sense for willpower to be the solution? If a man cannot conquer his own urges without God's help—should we be looking down on him when he fails? Blaming him for his wrongdoing? No, willpower will never be the solution to addiction. If there is a solution, it has to be something else.

The Nature of the Disease

Before we can look at the solution to addiction, we might want to sharpen how we understand the problem. Alcoholics Anonymous defines addiction as having three aspects.

1. *Addiction is physical.* In other words, alcoholics and addicts have a physical compulsion to keep on drinking or using long after the non-addict or non-alcoholic, the rational person, would stop. Where a normal person might hit a point of satiation, when an addict starts using his or her drug of choice, they feel physically compelled to keep going. Alcoholics and addicts typically drink or use until they run out of money, pass out, are arrested, or run out of friends who will pay for their alcohol or drugs.

   This is the physical component of addiction, which explains why the first spoonful of ice cream leads to wiping out the entire container, and why the first hit of cocaine can lead to a binge that lasts for many days and nights.

2. *Addiction is mental.* The mental component of addiction means that addicts trust their substance or addictive behavior far more than they trust other people. Let's face it: people will say no. They will tell you to stop doing what you're doing. They won't give you money. They'll divorce you. They'll throw you out of school. They'll arrest you. Under certain

circumstances, they'll even kill you. In short, you don't know what people will do.

By contrast, you always know what your substance or behavior of choice will do. It will take you out of the pain. You can count on Budweiser, or cocaine, or the internet, or the donut shop. Donuts and dime bags never say no. That's why addicts don't trust their loved ones, their employers, or even their drug dealers. Because they know at some point, the axe is going to fall. That's the mental aspect of addiction: trusting the substance or behavior more than they trust their family or friends.

3. *Addiction is spiritual.* Combine the physical and mental aspects of addiction and you end up with what Alcoholics Anonymous calls *the spiritual loss of values.* We all know what values are—they are the principles by which we distinguish between right and wrong. We learned our values from our parents, our teachers, our rabbeim, our roshei yeshivot, our older siblings, our coaches, or from people who are older and wiser and model appropriate behavior.

Addiction is called "the great eraser." As addicts become more and more sold out to their substance, everything else starts to take a backseat. Slowly, the addiction wipes out every concept of right and wrong, every value, except for the value of getting your fix.

For Jews thinking normally, life is about being honest, having integrity, giving tzedakah, supporting the community, building a family, staying connected to tradition, and so on. For the Orthodox, you can add studying Torah and observing the mitzvot. But if you're an addict, all that falls away. All those spiritual values you grew up with lose their meaning. That's why "If you loved me, why won't you stop?" doesn't work. Love is a value. The addict is essentially a slave to his addiction and will transgress every other principle to serve it.

So What's the Cure?

It should be clear by now that for a disease of this magnitude—one which consumes a person physically, mentally, and spiritually—the cure is not going to be a simple "stop cold turkey" sort of thing. And while we're at it, we can point out a few other things which are also not going to cure the addiction. For instance—shaming, guilt-tripping, arguing, punishing, goading, or even ever-so-sweetly encouraging an alcoholic to stop using—will generally have no effect, or a harmful effect, by giving the addict an excuse to use even more.

In AA, they talk about the difference between being "dry" and being "sober." Being "dry" means you're not using your substance. "Dry" is actually a pejorative term—a person who continues to act like an angry alcoholic even though she is no longer drinking alcohol is called a "dry drunk." By contrast, being sober means you've cleaned up all the other aspects of your life as an addict. You've learned to be responsible, you treat people properly, you pay what you owe, and generally live in an upstanding and honest way. Getting to a place of true sobriety when you've been living with addiction requires a heck of a lot more than just stopping using. On the flip side, to stop using, and to stop using *consistently*, usually requires more than just throwing the bottle away. Without getting "sober" in the larger sense, it is awfully hard to stay stopped.

True, an addict can sometimes stay stopped for a period of time, in order to finish a semester's worth of exams, complete a business deal, or demonstrate a period of sobriety to a spouse or a parole officer. But inevitably, the house of cards collapses, because that's what houses of cards do. So if willpower isn't the answer, then what is the cure for this terrible and often deadly disease? The mechanism that restores the power of choice to the addict or alcoholic is faith in God.

Remarkably, pretty much the only thing that has brought back large numbers of alcoholics and addicts from their disease is what Alcoholics Anonymous calls a "spiritual awakening." This awakening happens when, instead of relying on their own efforts to overcome the impulse to drink or use, addicts invite God into their lives to assist them. It sounds crazy. It sounds unlikely. But it's true.

We saw that addiction has a physical component—the desire to keep on drinking or using when a normal person would say, "I'm starting to feel it," and then stop. We have seen that there is a mental component as well, the sense that alcohol or drugs, porn, and food can be trusted, while people may let you down. And then, we saw that the combination of the physical compulsion to drink or use, combined with the mental obsession with one's drug of choice, leads to a spiritual loss of values.

When we look at all these features, we see a kind of enslavement. The entire person becomes dependent on the substance or behavior to which he or she is addicted. As we know from Jewish tradition, slavery is a kind of spiritual alienation or spiritual emptiness. And what kind of solution do we need for a spiritual problem like this? Not surprisingly, a spiritual one.

When the Jews were slaves in Egypt, the solution was not for them to pull themselves up by their bootstraps and swim across the Red Sea to safety. Rather, they needed to cry out to God, and He needed to respond to them with wonders and miracles that allowed them to leave. True, the Jews played a role along the way. They had to show that they were willing to trust God and to show that they were willing to do His will. But He was the rescuer.

The same is true with alcoholism and addiction. Yes, the addict has to take certain actions toward sobriety. He must ask God for help and seek to understand and do God's will. But if you're asking, "What can keep an alcoholic or addict from drinking or using?" The answer, to put it simply, is God.

But Don't Jews Already Know God?

One of the first responses to the idea that addicts need more God in their lives is, "But don't we already live spiritual lives as Jews? Don't we already have a connection to God?"

The answer, as is so often the case in Judaism, is yes and no. Many, if not most, Jews have a conflicted attitude toward God. On the one hand, God is the Being to whom many of us offer prayers each day or every week or, for some, realistically, maybe it's once a year on the high holidays. No matter how often we pray, at some level, all affiliated Jews acknowledge God as the Creator of the world, the Being that keeps the world turning, with light following darkness and darkness following light. Some of us have a sense of God's divine providence, which directs even the smallest details of the lives of every human being. Sounds good, right?

At the same time, we Jews don't submit easily to God's kingship. It's hard for us, on a practical level, to *surrender* to God, by committing to doing His will. And it's hard for us, on a practical level, to *trust* in God, by setting aside our anxiety about life, putting our next foot forward, and believing things will be all right.

We also struggle to accept God's plan, however, it manifests in our lives. We get upset when things don't go our way instead of adopting the mindset championed in the Mishnah, (Brachot, 9:5): *Bechol midah u'midah she'Hu moded lecha, hevei modeh lo bi'meod, meod*—With every measure and measure that He measures out to you, you shall be thankful to Him exceedingly.

We might say that we have in Judaism what the technology people call a "last mile" problem. With technology, it's easy to blanket the world in 5G coverage, but how do we ensure that every single home has access to the internet or other communications and media? We have to get access along the "last mile"—or whatever the distance is from the main server to the individual home. In technology, the last mile is the hardest. In Judaism, it's pretty much the same thing. It's one thing to understand *intellectually* that God created the world, that God keeps the world running, that God is responsible for day-to-day events, and that nothing happens without God's permission or awareness. It's fine to acknowledge these core beliefs through davening repeatedly throughout the day. But it's another thing entirely to travel that "last mile" or last foot or so—more accurately, from the head to the heart. It's one thing to accept intellectually if that's your religious belief, that God's in charge. It's another thing altogether for those who accept the idea of the existence and authority of God to accept on a heart level, to accept emotionally, that they can trust God with their lives.

This is a theoretical question for most people. Maybe you run into issues here or there and realize that having a more connected relationship with the Creator might be a good idea. But it isn't theoretical for the addict or alcoholic who wishes to stop drinking or using. Without finding a way to trust God, these people are trapped.

Currently, the most successful treatment for addiction is the twelve-step model pioneered by Alcoholics Anonymous. Others have found success with therapy, drugs, or other approaches, but AA is the mainstay when it comes to recovery. And the core idea behind AA and its progeny, the more than two hundred other Anonymous programs that deal with everything from smoking cessation to overeating, is the idea of turning one's entire being over to the care of God. If the addict or alcoholic can succeed at bringing God into his life, he might just be able to get his life back. If he can't—he's got three other options in the long run: institutions, insanity, or death.

Given those alternatives, recovery is starting to look pretty good. Does it have to happen with AA or another Anonymous group? Maybe it doesn't. But if you're looking to travel that last mile, and really bring God into your life on a personal level, it certainly pays to join up with some people who've been working on and succeeding at that for the past ninety years. Who have systematized this otherwise spiritual process and tailored it to the specific needs of alcoholics and addicts.

Still doubtful? That's okay.

Let's learn more about this spiritual cure for addiction and how it came to be.

In the next chapter.

CHAPTER 7

What Is Alcoholics Anonymous, and Is It Legit for Jews?

Some people refer to Bill Wilson as a stockbroker or a Wall Streeter, but in many ways, they're being too kind. Bill was essentially a stock speculator in the late 1920s, making paper fortunes as did everyone else in that overcaffeinated era, and then losing it all when the stock market crashed in 1929. He had made his initial stake when he piled his wife and some manuals about companies traded on the New York Stock Exchange into his Harley and went traveling around the southeastern United States.

He and his wife Lois would stop at a campground or an inexpensive motel near a factory. Bill would go hang around the bars where the employees would go after their shifts, and Bill would glean inside information about the future of these companies. Was business good? Did the future look bright? Were they hiring or laying off? What new products were coming online? Bill would turn that information into reports, which he would send back to broker friends on Wall Street, who would make investments based on Bill's guidance. When the stocks of the winners Bill picked went up, they would cut Bill in on profits. In some ways, Bill was the country's first stock analyst.

Bill had achieved success in other areas prior to his forays on Wall Street. He was a decorated World War I veteran, had completed law school at night (although he never picked up his diploma), and had even been offered a job by the great Thomas Edison himself, although Bill turned the job down. He had an intense, burning desire to be the "number-one man" but he couldn't decide in what field he wanted to be number one. And along the way, he drank, and he drank, and he drank.

The drinking affected his ability to earn a living, and the couple relied on the income Lois brought home as a sales clerk in a department store. Bill wrote later that he would rob his wife's "slender purse" for money for booze. In the early 1930s, after the market crashed, Bill was hospitalized repeatedly for alcoholism. He would dry out, swear off, and inevitably resume his drinking. Lois was appalled, yet she never left Bill. Those were the times, and that was her nature.

In the fall of 1934, Bill was sitting alone in their Brooklyn apartment, most likely drinking, when a friend from his small hometown in Vermont, Ebby Thatcher, came to visit. Bill was delighted because Ebby drank the way he did, so the old friends could tie one on together. There was only one problem. Ebby had stopped drinking.

"I've got religion," Ebby announced, and Bill was aghast. But he let Ebby stay nonetheless and share his message of recovery from alcoholism.

Ebby told Bill that he had fallen under the sway of an organization known as Oxford Group, an international movement also known as Moral Re-Armament, launched by an MD named Frank Buchman. In the wake of the destruction of the First World War, the Oxford Group wanted nothing more than world peace. At the same time, while they were trying to reform the world's politics, the group also developed an interest in reforming alcoholics, of all people. The Oxford Group had what it called "drunk squads"—individuals who would work with alcoholics and try to convince them that their drinking was killing them.

Bill's old friend Ebby had encountered members of the Oxford Group who had convinced him to stop drinking by turning to God for help. The individual responsible for Ebby's religious conversion, if that's not too strong a term, was a fellow Oxford Grouper named Rowland Hazard. Roland was a well-to-do American businessman who had tried all sorts of different approaches to cure his own alcoholism, all of which ended in failure. Rowland had the means, so he actually upped and went to Switzerland for a year to be treated by none other than the famous therapist and author Carl Jung. At the end of the year's treatment, Jung sadly informed Roland that there was nothing in psychology that could keep a man from living as an alcoholic.

Rowland despaired, and Jung explained that the only thing he had ever seen work with alcoholics was a complete reordering of their spiritual lives. Rowland, armed with that information, joined the Oxford Group, where he found people willing to work with him and show him a path to God that would allow him to stop drinking. So we see the chain of progression from Carl Jung to Rowland to Ebby Thatcher to Bill Wilson, who found himself deeply affected by Ebby's cessation of drinking.

Specifically, Ebby shared with Bill the Oxford Group idea that Bill could choose his own conception of God. Instead of being told, "This is who God is and this is what you must do," Bill could direct his thoughts and prayers to his own God concept, who would then relieve Bill of his alcoholism.

After the encounter with Ebby, Bill ended up drinking yet again, so much so that he ended up in Towns Hospital, a drying-out establishment for the well-to-do on Manhattan's Central Park West. During this hospitalization, in December 1934, Bill cried out bitterly, "If there is a God, let Him show Himself!" The room filled with white light, he later claimed, and he experienced the presence of God as he had never experienced it before. The head of the hospital, Charlie Towns, visited him and realized that something had happened to Bill. From that moment in 1934 to Bill's death in 1971, he never drank again.

Bill was so excited by his conversion experience that he spent the next six months proselytizing to drunks wherever he could find them—in bars, on the street, anywhere. Exactly zero alcoholics followed him in his quest for sobriety through spirituality. After six months, he told his wife of his disappointment over his inability to convince others to quit drinking. He saw his whole experiment as a failure. That's when Lois pointed out the obvious—that for the first time in his adult life, Bill had not picked up a drink. He was stone-cold sober.

Bill went back to the hospital where he got sober and had a conversation with the MD there, Charles Silkworth. Dr. Silkworth suggested that Bill modify his approach. Instead of preaching to drunks about the ills of drinking, he should talk about his own story and how he was able to stop. Bill liked the idea. Not long thereafter, he found himself in Akron, Ohio, sent there by his stalwart friends on Wall Street to run a proxy campaign to take over a particular business enterprise. The campaign failed, and Bill found himself on a Sunday in June 1935 in Akron, Ohio, with nothing to do until he could get back to New York. He was staying at the Mayflower Hotel, and the only excitement in the hotel, and presumably in Akron, was in the hotel bar, a place where Bill knew he had no business. So Bill took a series of actions, seemingly small and insignificant, which, in many ways, would ultimately change the world.

He went to the payphone, started dropping in nickels, and called ministers from the adjacent framed list of contact information for churches. He explained to whichever surprised minister he could interrupt from Sunday lunch that he was an alcoholic from New York. He was looking for some local alcoholics he could work with and with whom he could share his message of sobriety. Not surprisingly, the first nine ministers thought he was a crank or a kook and quickly ended the call. But Bill was persistent, and he finally made the tenth call to a minister by the name of Ernest Tunks.

"Do you know any alcoholics?" Bill asked Reverend Tunks.

"I might just," Tunks replied and connected Bill with a woman named Henrietta Seiberling the heiress to an Akron tire fortune.

Are you still with me?

Henrietta Seiberling explained to Bill that a doctor friend, a proctologist named Bob Smith, had a terrible drinking problem and perhaps Bill could speak with Bob. Bill agreed to come over to the guest house on her estate where Bob was living, but Bob was too drunk to talk to Bill, so they rescheduled for the next day. Bob thought it absurd that a failed Wall Streeter had anything useful to tell him about alcoholism since he, of course, was a trained physician. So, he agreed to give Bill fifteen minutes.

Those fifteen minutes stretched into a conversation lasting six hours or more. Because Bill was able to speak so frankly of his own alcoholism, Bob realized that this was a kindred spirit, someone who understood him. And because Bob, like Bill, was a churchgoer and a believer, he was able to accept without too much difficulty Bill's notion that a spiritual approach could arrest alcoholism. Bill Wilson and Dr. Bob Smith are considered the cofounders of what became Alcoholics Anonymous, and that six-hour meeting was the first conversation between the two men.

Dr. Bob wasn't quite done drinking, however. He went off to attend the American Medical Association conference a couple of weeks later in Atlantic City, New Jersey and got loaded on the train ride home. The day of Dr. Bob's last drink, June 15, 1935, was later established as the founding day of Alcoholics Anonymous. Dr. Bob would live another sixteen years and never went back to the bottle in all that time.

When Dr. Bob told people in his hospital in Akron that he had found a cure for alcoholism, they asked him whether he might consider taking it himself. He had that one coming. Bill was so excited to have a real, live person who accepted his ideas and his methodology that he stayed on in Akron, and Bob and Bill began to sober up other alcoholics who had been admitted to the hospital where Dr. Bob worked.

The third member of the then-unnamed group was a hospital patient also named Bill, called Bill D. in AA lore so as to distinguish him from Bill Wilson. Bill D. was described as "a corker" who had "just beaten up a couple of nurses. Goes off his head completely when he's drinking. But he's a grand chap when he's sober, though he's been in here eight times in the last six months. Understand he was once a well-known lawyer in town, but just now we've got him strapped down tight."

Bill and Dr. Bob made their pitch to Bill D., known to later generations of AA as "the man on the bed." Bill D. pondered their message over the course of the next day. He enjoyed the luxury of doing it in the single room to which Dr. Bob had moved him. Bill D. was no stranger to the drunk ward at the hospital. The next morning, when Bill and Bob came back, Bill D. signed on. He got dressed and went home, never to drink again. The three of them began to carry their message, first through the local Oxford Group and then through AA talks in the Akron area.

After a couple of years of this work, the men did the math. Although they had spoken to hundreds of individuals, as many as fifty or sixty had actually gotten sober and remained sober for any meaningful period of time. Bill, still plagued by delusions of grandeur and the desire to be the "number-one man," saw this nascent organization as something that might spread nationwide, with hospitals, drying-out clinics, and other for-profit enterprises. The humble name he proffered as the group's moniker: The Bill W. Society.

Cooler heads prevailed, and Bill was talked out of turning what was to become AA into a money-making venture. On the other hand, the others did agree with Bill that it would be a good idea to put out a book so that doctors across the country could explain the spiritual remedy for alcoholism to their patients. The organization still had no name, however, and neither did the book. It looked for a long time as though the book would be called *The Way Out*, but then a search revealed that there were at least a dozen other books by the same name. Finally, at a meeting to discuss the book, one of the members just said, "Why don't you just call it *Alcoholics Anonymous*, period?" So now, the book, which is also known as the *Big Book of Alcoholics Anonymous*, as well as the organization, got its name.

There's more to the story, of course, but that's essentially how AA started. Today, somewhere between a million and two million recovering alcoholics attend AA meetings worldwide, and probably another million people belong to twelve-step fellowships like Overeaters Anonymous, Smokers Anonymous, Cocaine Anonymous, Marijuana Anonymous, and Al-Anon family groups, which serve family members of alcoholics.

AA humbly insists that it does not possess a hammerlock on treatment of alcoholism. In reality, however, it is hard to find other methods with the consistent success that AA has had. Treatment centers and rehabs exist to give those seeking recovery the ability to get away from the people, places, and things that trigger their use of alcohol, drugs, and other substances and behaviors. Yet most treatment centers focus on the twelve steps of Alcoholics Anonymous and have their residents take at least the first three, if not all twelve steps, while still in residence.

Other people have tried to come up with other answers to alcohol addiction. About twenty years ago, a woman in Washington state created a group called Moderation Management that permitted moderate drinking, which differs from the AA model of complete abstinence. She shied away from the term "alcoholic," which apparently did not feel like a comfortable way to describe herself. Instead, she spoke of "problem drinkers," a term that she admitted applied to her.

Unfortunately, the founder of Moderation Management found moderation a goal too hard to achieve. One day while perhaps aiming for moderate drinking, she instead got loaded, drove her car in an alcoholic blackout, and killed a father and his twelve-year-old daughter. The Moderation Management story suggests that AA is correct that only abstinence, not moderation, works for alcoholics and addicts. Milton Dicus, a mentor of mine, used to say that "Alcoholics don't taper off; they taper on."

Another alternative to AA is the medicines that cause alcoholics to become violently ill if they drink alcohol. The only problem is that they don't like throwing up. So they stop taking the medicine.

Many addicts and alcoholics prefer to go the therapy route, talking over their alcoholism and addictions with a psychologist or a psychiatrist. Some professionals have guided their patients to stop drinking and using. Yet most point out that therapy is often pointless unless the patient stops drinking and using, and the most effective way to stop drinking and using is by going to AA.

So, to date, AA is the most effective treatment for addiction and alcoholism. Which brings us to our next challenge— getting Jews to feel comfortable about going to Alcoholics Anonymous. As we saw earlier, due to the stigma and silence around addiction in Jewish communities, there are seemingly endless reasons why Jews don't want to go to any kind of treatment. And AA is at the bottom of the list of things they're willing to try! A lot of Jews simply don't like the idea of Alcoholics Anonymous. They think it's too Christian, they think it's weird, and they think that their privacy will be compromised because people will see them in the meetings.

So what's a person who wants to stop using and drinking to do? Go or not go? The best way to answer that question is to explain how AA works, what the process of recovery is all about, and why an unending series of rabbinical authorities have determined that AA is legit for Jews.

CHAPTER 8

Is AA Kosher for Jews?

S uppose you or someone you know has a life-threatening disease. Currently, the only cure with a track record of success happens to have been developed by a Christian doctor and is usually only available in Christian hospitals. Are you allowed to attend the Christian hospital (they have a policy to not ask you to accept Jesus into your heart!) in order to receive this life-saving cure? Perhaps more importantly, are you allowed *not to* attend this hospital, out of Jewish pride or religious zealotry, if it means you are putting your life at risk?

This is our first question when we look at AA from a Jewish perspective. Not whether it's a cult, or it's a problem that meetings are often in churches, or if we can go to meetings with non-Jews. These questions are all secondary. The first question is, given that addiction is a life-threatening disease and that AA is the best-known cure to date, do we have permission, as life-affirming Jews, not to use it?

Protecting life is the highest priority in Jewish tradition. For those in the Orthodox framework, we all know that there are only three circumstances when we can set this priority aside—to avoid adultery, to avoid idolatry, and to avoid murder. AA does not involve any of those cardinal three, which means that if it has the potential to save a life, using it should not be an issue. Understandably, however, Jews are hesitant about participating in AA for several reasons. And we can address those reasons, one by one. But the bottom line is that we're talking about a disease that left unchecked takes lives and destroys families.

Why Is Judaism Not Enough?

Now, if the spiritual solution for alcoholism and addiction could be activated by davening three times a day, or by any other religious method, the solution to addiction would be Orthodoxy, and there would be no addiction in the observant Jewish community. Since this isn't the case, a somewhat different path to God must be found.

As we mentioned, the problem with religious ritual and observance is that we can still end up with a "last mile" problem. Connecting emotionally to what we believe intellectually is just really hard. Especially in Judaism, it can be easy to get caught up in the externals of our practice: high holiday services, the Pesach seder, lighting the Menorah, and, for the more religious, the countless daily practices that religious life demands.

Many addicts who grew up religious expressed that while they were practicing Jews, they never felt they had a real connection with God. Judaism might still have been a meaningful way to connect with family and with community—but God was a remote and unknown force, with no direct presence in their lives. One benefit of AA is to remove the shame and anger people may feel when contemplating the idea of God. So AA actually helps people find their way back to religion.

AA's Jewish Roots

The two men who co-founded Alcoholics Anonymous, Bill Wilson and Dr. Bob Smith, were both Christian. The language of the basic text of AA—the *Big Book* and the secondary text, *AA's Twelve Steps and Twelve Traditions*—has a Christian, mid-century feel at times. But once you start digging even slightly beneath the surface, a different picture appears. The voice may at times be the voice of Christianity, but the ideas are 100 percent consistent with Jewish thought. At its core, there is nothing in Alcoholics Anonymous that disqualifies it for a religious or secular Jew.

What might get some Jews a bit uncomfortable are the prayers that are occasionally recited within an AA meeting. Some were suggested by AA's co-founder Bill Wilson. Others are the Serenity Prayer and, in some meetings, the Lord's Prayer. You don't actually have to *say* these prayers if you are uncomfortable with them. In fact, you don't *have* to do anything you don't want to do. You don't have to speak. You don't have to say your name. You don't have to say, "I'm so and so and I'm an alcoholic." You can just, as the AA expression goes, fill a seat. Listen and learn. So you can skip the prayer parts if you want to.

But would it be a problem to say these prayers if you wanted to? Highly unlikely. Some AA meetings, although fewer and fewer these days, end with a recitation of the Lord's Prayer. It reads as follows:

> Our Father, who art in Heaven, hallowed be
> Thy name; Thy kingdom come; Thy will be
> done on earth as it is in heaven. Give us this
> day our daily bread; and forgive us our tres-
> passes as we forgive those who trespass against
> us; and lead us not into temptation, but deliver
> us from evil. Amen.

Christian, you say? Our Father who art in Heaven and so on? Try this on for size: *Avinu shebashamayim.* Sounds pretty Jewish to me. Which means…wait for it…"Our Father who art in Heaven." But you knew that already.

If we keep going line by line, it is a prayer that any mono-theistic person can easily get behind. We ask God's will to be done, for God to provide for our needs and forgive us for our mistakes, and to save us from temptation. You can find those themes all over your Jewish siddur.

Then there's the Serenity Prayer, which was composed by the Christian theologian Reinhold Niebuhr in the first half of the 20th century. This prayer is fairly well known:

> God, grant me the serenity to accept the things I
> cannot change, the courage to change the things
> I can, and the wisdom to know the difference.

Nothing doctrinal about that, is there?

Sometimes you will hear the St. Francis Prayer, which is pleasant enough and has no doctrinally Christian or non-Jewish aspect to it.

Lord, make me an instrument of Your peace.
Where there is hatred, let me bring love.
Where there is offence, let me bring pardon.
Where there is discord, let me bring union.
Where there is error, let me bring truth.
Where there is doubt, let me bring faith.
Where there is despair, let me bring hope...etc.

And then, there are the two prayers that Bill Wilson suggested, which go along with Steps Three and Seven. These prayers are nondenominational and entirely optional. In short, all AA "liturgy" is strictly nondenominational. You don't have to say it, but even if you did, you wouldn't be violating your Judaism.

The Twelve Steps

When Bill Wilson was writing the basic text of AA in 1938, he took the six principles of the Oxford Group, which that organization set forth as a means of spiritual growth, and expanded them to twelve concepts. Those are the famous Twelve Steps, a process through which newcomers go to attain the spiritual awakening that offers the best possible safeguard against relapse. I'll take you through the Twelve Steps later in this book, but for now, let's break them down into four basic categories, based on the terminology offered by AA co-founder Dr. Bob Smith, the proctologist we met earlier, and see how they jive with being Jewish.

1. *Surrender*

The first category is known in Alcoholics Anonymous and other Anonymous programs as surrender. Here, we admit to, or surrender, in slightly more dramatic language, to the fact that we have a problem with alcohol, drugs, or another addictive or compulsive behavior or substance. We acknowledge that spiritual help is available, which is simply a way of saying that we don't need to solve this all by ourselves. And then we agree to let God help us with our addiction problem.

Is this a Jewish idea? We've already seen that the Jewish view of free choice is not as all-encompassing as we might have thought. The consequence? To take advantage of God's willingness to help us, we *have* to surrender in some way. As the great psalmist writes, "Cast your burden on the LORD and He will sustain you" (Psalms 55:23).

Now, one of the key terms in Alcoholics Anonymous and other twelve-step programs is "higher power." This term can be a turn-off to Jews because we have our own names for God. When the Steps were written, allowance had to be made for atheists and agnostics who also suffered from drinking problems. Endless debate took place in the early days of AA, with some factions arguing against the spiritual solution and calling for a more humanistic approach and others believing that God had to be at the center of recovery or nothing would work. Finally, the phrase "higher power" was used to indicate to the members that they could choose any concept of a creator or higher being that they liked.

The goal of this language was to give a spiritual push to the program while respecting every member's right to participate in their religion, believe what they believe, and call God whatever they like to call God in their faith. The term "higher power," or a "power greater than ourselves," was offered as a term that would be acceptable to everyone, including those who did not like the term "God."

The English word "God" doesn't sound Jewish. We call God *Hashem*, *HaKadosh Barch Hu*, or *Abishter*, all of which are Hebrew or Yiddish, and feel Jewish.

But when it comes to the "higher power" terminology, if someone has an issue with how it sounds—my response is to get over it. You're dying of an alcohol or cocaine addiction, you've trashed your marriage, your career is in shambles, you're looking at jail time, or your kids caught you watching porn, and you're taking exception to the term "higher power?" Seriously?

2. *Introspection*

Dr. Bob called the next four Steps "Introspection." These steps are about self-examination. This is where we find out who we really are (spoiler alert: we're all beautiful children of God), and this is where we invite God into our lives at an even deeper level, to help us correct our moral failings to become the people we were always meant to be.

Is this kind of introspection a Jewish idea? Of course. For one, we pretty much invented the "image of God" self-esteem concept that AA uses so much to its advantage. You'll hear echoes of this concept all over Jewish thought and teaching. On top of that, one of the most famous books studied in Orthodox communities is *The Path of the Just* or *Mesillat*

Yesharim. This little book presents for its readers a step-by-step path to moral perfection. You know what the first few steps are? Introspection and self-examination to correct our moral failings.

While we retain self-esteem by remembering that we are beautiful children of God, we start to correct our mistakes by taking a moral inventory and seeing whether we are living up to our ideals. Now, you might be surprised that addicts are even capable of a moral inventory. However, though an addict's family members may believe that the addict has no conscience, based on the way he or she is acting, the conscience of the addict is never fully anesthetized. They may not realize what they're doing during an alcohol- or drug-induced blackout, but when they come to, and they survey the wreckage to themselves, to their finances, to their loved ones, they are incredibly angry and disappointed with themselves, which, of course, triggers a necessity to drink and use even more.

So while the purpose of the fourth through seventh Steps is certainly about recognizing the behavioral or character flaws of the addict or alcoholic, they also exist to remind the addict that he or she is still a beautiful child of God, created in God's image, and therefore valuable. The more this sinks in, the more the addict will be able to do that *Path of the Just*-style character development.

3. *Restitution*

Now come the next two Steps, Eight and Nine, which are about restitution. This is where members make lists of people they have harmed and then apologize to those individuals. There's a lot of guidance about when, whether, and how to make these amends, as these apologies are called in the twelve-step vernacular.

The basic idea is that if you're trying to awaken your spirit, it's tough to do so if you haven't set right the wrongs you've done, whether to family members, community members, employers, or yourself. In other words, *Sur mei'rah, va'asei tov*—Turn from evil and do good (Psalms 34:15). You have to stop your bad behaviors before you can start living an upstanding life.

This amends-making sure sounds a lot like the teshuvah process, doesn't it? We're told that when it comes to the harm that we've caused *bein adam l'echavero*, between us and our fellow human beings, we have no business asking God for forgiveness until we ask directly the person we've harmed. So, restitution in the twelve steps...what's un-Jewish about that?

4. *Maintenance*

And then come the final three Steps, which some people refer to as the "maintenance" Steps, but which are really about enhancing one's spiritual growth. In Dr. Bob's old-school AA terminology, these three Steps boil down to the word "witness" which, I admit, sounds a little Christian. In this sense, to "witness" is to share one's spiritual experience with another person. AA members believe that they cannot keep the gift of sobriety unless they share freely with others what they have discovered. So they are "witnessing" or, to put it more simply, showing to others that AA has managed to get them sober and keep them that way.

What these Steps are really about is demonstrating that you are indeed a changed person, that you are accountable for your behavior today, and that you are carrying a message of recovery to other suffering addicts. If you take the actions these Steps suggest, your spirit will reawaken. And when your spirit is awakened, you no longer feel the need to act out with alcohol, drugs, food, money, porn, or any of the other substances and behaviors addicts use so often to kill their pain.

If Abraham was the first person to "recover" from an issue (paganism), then these last Steps were what he did once he changed his life. He continually demonstrated his commitment to God, while welcoming all others into his tent and sharing with them this new way of understanding the world under monotheism. Likewise, addicts are encouraged to not stop with their own recovery, but to take part in assisting others. In fact, you will find a level of selfless devotion between members of twelve-step programs that is rare to find elsewhere.

That level of camaraderie and selflessness is rare, even in the Jewish community. But is it supposed to be? Or is that supposed to be the norm? The final Steps of AA, without a doubt, push forward the Jewish moral vision in profound and meaningful ways.

Is AA a Cult?

We've all seen eerie documentaries or news stories about cults. Groups of people led by a charismatic leader who manipulates his or her followers into giving up their bodies, their freedom, their money—or all the above—and dedicating them to the "cause." Scientology has been revealed in recent years to have a cult-like mentality, continually demanding the highest levels of devotion and donations from its followers, separating family members from one another, while abusing them physically and psychologically. I think we can all agree that it is a good policy to stay away from cults.

Some people imagine that Alcoholics Anonymous might have cultish tendencies. Fortunately, that could not be further from the truth. AA describes itself as a "fellowship," an informal group or series of groups of individuals who declare themselves to be, at any given moment, members. There are no dues, fees, or membership requirements (other than the desire to stop drinking). They pass a basket at most meetings, and most people kick in a dollar or three dollars, to defray the costs of the meeting—rent, coffee, cleaning supplies, and AA literature. There are no contracts to sign. There is no long-term commitment.

AA describes itself as "the last house on the block," where you go when you've got nowhere else to go. You don't have to lose everything in order to join Alcoholics Anonymous, but it can be harder to believe that you've really run out of options with two cars in the garage and money in the bank. Some people who come to Alcoholics Anonymous have blown through considerable wealth before they got there. Others had nothing before they arrived and are building solid financial lives for the first time, now that they are sober. As they say in AA, it doesn't matter if you went to Yale or jail, if you slept in Park Place or on a park bench. All that matters is that you are here now.

If AA were a cult, it would "recruit" new members *before* they lost everything, it would have them sign a contract, and it would try to separate them from loved ones instead of trying to bring marriages and families back together. As a result, it would be something other than what it actually is—a loosely confederated, minimally organized entity under whose broad auspices meetings take place around the world.

Many Jews are concerned that some AA meetings take place in churches, and that therefore AA must have some sort of Christian bias or feel. The reason AA meetings take place in churches is that churches have meeting space and are willing to rent out that space to AA and other twelve-step groups. The group gets a place to meet, while the church gets rent and gets to feel useful. Everybody wins. In virtually no cases is there any tie between church dogma or church management and the independent, autonomous AA meeting renting space from it.

AA meetings don't just take place in churches. They also take place in temples, in banks, on beaches, in schools, in hospitals, in libraries, and even in courthouses. A meeting that takes place in a Charlestown, Massachusetts, courthouse is known as the "You Be The Judge" meeting. So it's possible to attend AA meetings on a regular basis without setting foot on church property.

True Mutual Respect

In today's world, we're used to there being an agenda. If you live on the coasts, the agenda is political, if you live in between, it might be religious. So it's hard for us to believe there could be an organization that provides so much, demands so little, and doesn't push its members to think or believe a certain way. But believe it, my friend, because it's true.

Some members of twelve-step programs have always participated in or, once sober, returned to the religions of their childhood. Others do not partake in religion at all. One of the Traditions or core tenets of Alcoholics Anonymous is to leave the question of religious participation to individual members. In fact, AA's tradition asks people to refrain from discussing the things that may separate members from each other and divert them from their common task—remaining sober and helping others achieve their sobriety. These divisive topics include politics, religion, profession, and financial status. Are you rich? Great, but try not to mention it at an AA meeting, where nobody cares.

The focus is supposed to be on recovery and sobriety, which is the common thread binding all AA members, as opposed to topics that might cause factionalism. AA learned from the choice a 19th-century temperance group, the Washingtonians, made, when they got caught up in political issues and subsequently fell apart.

You will seldom hear a political opinion expressed in an AA meeting, and, if so, the speaker will receive guidance, usually in private, from a long-standing member to avoid continuing to make such comments in the future.

A Place for All People

One turn-off for some Jews is AA's wide-ranging attendance. And it's true, you will meet all types in an AA meeting. Some people in AA call themselves "low-bottom drunks" because they lost everything and ended up living on the street.[20] Others experienced relatively high bottoms—they came into

---

[20]   Or on the beach. One Los Angeles AA member describes living on the beach as a "sandominium."

AA still possessed of their homes, their cars, their jobs, their family, and their faculties.

If you peer around the room in a twelve-step meeting, you may also come to the unavoidable conclusion that 5 to 10 percent of the people in the room are Jews. Surprise! You're not alone. You aren't Christopher Columbus, sailing off the end of the planet, encountering people you think are Indians. Instead, a meaningful minority of the people you'll encounter in AA meetings are lantzmen, unless you're in someplace like Albuquerque or Cheyenne. But you'll likely find some yiddin in the meetings there, too.

Keep in mind that joining Alcoholics Anonymous, or any other twelve-step program, is hard for *everybody*, not just Jews. Young people come into the rooms and see a lot of old people and say, "I can wait a couple of decades and try this later." (There now exist "Young People's Meetings" comprising people from their teens to their thirties for this very reason.) Women come in and say, "Hey it's mostly men, I don't belong." Blacks come in and say, "It's too white." Professionals come in and say, "Everybody here is blue-collar." So it's not as though the Jew entering an AA meeting is the only one who feels out of place. All members are stepping outside their normal social milieu—whether that milieu is the upper echelons of society, your Catholic Hispanic community, or your hip millennial friends.

You don't need to be like the people around you to benefit from the recovery process. Newcomers are invited to see if they identify with the feelings, not compare their addictive journey or their life journey with those of the speakers! In other words, the only binding factor among members of a twelve-step program is their struggle with their addiction, and their effort to overcome it.

If you were sitting in a lifeboat and needed to row to shore, you would no doubt take up an oar next to any man sitting beside you—whether he was Christian, Moslem, black, Latino, young, old—you name it. That's the camaraderie of the AA groups. Just a bunch of people working together to row to shore.

***

So, is AA kosher for Jews? Is a life-saving cure that puts people in touch with God in a completely non-coercive or proselytizing way something that we can comfortably engage in and still feel okay about our Jewishness? I hope you'll agree the answer is yes.

In fact, not only is AA kosher for Jews, but many Jews testify to feeling more connected to their Judaism as a result of getting involved in a twelve-step program. As we've seen, these programs can actually *deepen* a Jew's commitment to Jewish practice. What could possibly be un-kosher about that?

CHAPTER 9

What It Means to Take the Steps

In this chapter, I'm going to speak in the first-person plural, as if I were representing AA, and the "you" to whom I am speaking stands for the alcoholic or addict in need of recovery[21]. Also, rather than keep on repeating the phrase *alcoholic or addict*, which would be tiresome, I'll speak of AA and alcoholism. You can plug in any addiction and any twelve-step program you like, and the results should be about the same.

The twelve steps of Alcoholics Anonymous, which have been modified for all the other 200+ twelve-step programs, are a series of suggested statements and actions, the purpose

---

[21] Please be sure that I am not authorized to speak on behalf of AA or to "represent" it in any formal matter. No one does. Instead, I use the term "represent" metaphorically, just to make the chapter flow more naturally.

of which is to reawaken the spirit of the alcoholic who wishes to stay clean and sober.

Interestingly, the word "alcohol" only appears in the first of the Twelve Steps. After that, the next eleven Steps have to do with creating and maintaining a way of life that points toward sobriety. Since the Twelve Steps were crafted in the late 1930s, the language has not changed, at least in Alcoholics Anonymous. Yet the means by which the Steps are "taken" or applied to the life of the alcoholic or addict have changed. So this chapter will talk about how the Steps were taken back in the day, how they are taken today, and what makes the most sense in terms of ensuring recovery.

Step 1: We admitted we were powerless over alcohol—that our lives had become unmanageable.

Step One consists of two phrases: *We admitted that we were powerless over alcohol—that our lives had become unmanageable.* Gallons of ink have been spilled analyzing these phrases. To keep it simple, they are assertions with which, ultimately, the alcoholic must agree in order to make a start in recovery.

We admitted we were powerless over alcohol. This is an admission of defeat. We might not have gotten drunk or in trouble every time we drank, but as time went on, it became clear that we could not drink in safety. We were unable to limit the amount of alcohol we consumed. We were unable to stop when we had promised ourselves or others that we would stop. Alcohol sometimes led to other behaviors in which we might not have indulged had we not been drinking. It's hard to drive drunk if you haven't been drinking. You're less likely to throw caution to the wind and call a drug dealer and order up some cocaine if you are sober. The same thing with any other addictive behavior.

Alcohol is the great loosener of inhibitions. If you start drinking, you don't know where you are going to end up. You are powerless. If you cannot stop when you intend to stop, you are powerless. If you are drinking more than you want to drink, if you're drinking with people who ordinarily would not drink, and if you're doing things that you might not normally do if you were not under the influence of alcohol, you're powerless.

Different people have different definitions. I knew a woman in AA who just needed a few puffs on a marijuana cigarette to get as high as a kite (lightweight, you're thinking). It doesn't matter how much you drank, it doesn't matter where you drank, it doesn't matter if you were drinking top-shelf booze or cheap rotgut. Or shaving lotion or Listerine, for that matter. All that matters is whether you were able to determine when you'd had enough. If you weren't, you're powerless, which means that you're in agreement with the first half of the first Step.

Our lives have become unmanageable. Unmanageable in this context means out of control. If your home life is out of control, if your work life is out of control, if your finances are out of control, if your ability to meet the demands of your religious life is out of control, then you are living in a state of unmanageability.

The dash that connects the two phrases essentially asks you to see a connection between drinking and the fact that your life is out of control. Steeped in denial, most alcoholics cannot see that connection. They see alcohol as the solution instead of the problem. This is why they aren't doing so well in life. Once you can make the connection between being powerless over alcohol and having an unmanageable life, you've taken Step One.

AA co-founder Bill Wilson wrote that the first and second Steps are up-or-down propositions. All you have to do is agree with them or disagree, and you've taken that Step. You can move on to the next one since the Steps were meant to be taken one at a time and in order. If you don't think that your life is unmanageable, if you still think you can control your alcohol, then you have what AA calls "reservations" about your alcoholism. Until you give up those reservations, you're likely to keep on drinking. So what's it going to be?

These days, sponsors typically ask newcomers to write a paragraph or sometimes an entire essay about why they think they are powerless over alcohol and why their lives are unmanageable. Back in the day, the newcomer started taking Steps as soon as he stopped throwing up. The newcomer's hand was too shaky to write and his hand was too fogged. Whether you write essays or simply nod your head in agreement, if you can buy the concepts of the two phrases in Step One, you've taken the Step. That's the problem. Now we move on to the solution, which is Step Two: *We came to believe that a power greater than ourselves could restore us to sanity.*

Step 2: Came to believe that a power greater than ourselves could restore us to sanity.

Most alcoholics and addicts bristle when they see the phrase "restored to sanity." That's because they don't like being told that they're insane. "Insane" is a Latin term for unhealthy. Tell me what's healthy about drinking or drugging to excess.

Tell me what's healthy about putting your life, your marriage, your children's lives, your financial life, your education, and your career at risk? Nothing. So you're trying to be restored to health.

The first few words, "came to believe," indicate that most alcoholics have a period of awakening on the way to recovery. They aren't buying in all at once to the idea that they have a problem. "If you stick around long enough in Alcoholics Anonymous," quotes Dr. Paul O., one of AA's most beloved longtime members,[22] "you'll catch alcoholism, because it's contagious in the rooms." I don't mean contagious like COVID-19. I mean contagious in the sense that when you hear other people talking about how alcohol affected them, you'll just come to say, *That's me. I have the same problem.*

Step Two can therefore be summed up this way: *came—*started showing up at AA meetings. *Came to—*realized that I was living life unconsciously, in the grips of my addiction without realizing it, and came to believe, gradually, over a period of time, that something could help me since my own willpower was failing.

Now we come to the all-important phrase, *a power greater than ourselves.* Spoiler alert: this means God. Early AA experience taught that newcomers were very excited to learn that there was a solution to alcoholism but were soon disappointed to discover that the solution was spiritual. And here it is: The signature idea of Alcoholics Anonymous is that alcoholics cannot rely on their own thinking to stay sober, but if they invite God to help them with their sobriety, they won't have to drink. It's a revolutionary idea, inspired

---

[22] Dr. Paul wrote the Acceptance paragraph found in the AA Big Book on page 419 (page 449 if you're old school).

by Dr. Jung and not universally accepted even within AA. Arguments abounded as to whether AA ought to be secular, not spiritual in nature.

But the co-founders, Bill and Dr. Bob won out, and you will hear AA members across the globe in meetings telling you that God keeps them sober, as unlikely as that may sound. This is not an easy idea for most people to accept. Those who have never had a relationship with God can be slow to take Step Two because they've never trusted God, thought they needed God, or prayed. Others looked at tragedies in the world or in their own lives and asked who could trust a God who permitted such misery. Some religious people also find this concept challenging. They have been praying all their lives, so why hasn't God helped them before?

This is actually a question that pertains to those of us who identify as Orthodox Jews, who pray three times daily and are constantly reciting blessings, studying, and otherwise keeping religion at the center of their lives. If you are already praying to a higher power, what does AA have to teach you?

What's different about spirituality in AA is that it asks its members to pray specifically for release from addiction. The thinking is that if we don't invite God specifically to solve the problem of addiction, He will wait until we do. Chuck C., an influential member of Alcoholics Anonymous from the 1940s on, wrote in his book, *A New Pair Of Glasses* (1984), "God is a gentleman. He doesn't go anywhere He isn't invited." It's one thing to daven for the rebuilding of Jerusalem or any of the other matters with which Jewish liturgy concerns itself. It's a separate matter to ask God specifically to relieve us of our alcoholism. That's what AA wants us to do. So now let's assemble the constituent parts of Step Two.

Came to believe that a power higher than ourselves could restore us to sanity is a late 1930s way of saying, "essentially bought the idea that there's a spiritual solution to my addiction problem." AA co-founder Bill Wilson describes the first two Steps as a "threefold admission"—powerless over alcohol; unmanageability of life; insanity. If you can accept the basic idea of Step Two, then your sponsor can sign you off on the Step and the two of you can begin work on Step Three.

Step 3: Made a decision to turn our will and our lives over to the care of God as we understood Him.

Let's take a look at the language of the Step to start things off:

> *We made a decision to turn our will and our lives over to the care of God as we understood Him.*

There are a lot of moving parts here, but at the core, AA members summarize the first three Steps this way: I can't (Step One), God can (Step Two), I'm going to let Him (Step Three). So what does that mean?

Made implies a moment of action. The word "decision" literally means to cut away, as in eliminating all possibilities other than the one that you've chosen. So when alcoholics make the decision to stop drinking, they are literally cutting away any possibility of returning to their addictive behavior.

Okay, we're making a decision. We're cutting away other options. What decision exactly are we making? Specifically, we are making a decision to turn our will and our lives over to God's care. What do we mean by our will and our lives?

The best answer I've seen comes from the pair of alcoholics from the American South, one white and one African-American, named Joe and Charlie. They toured the country putting on multiday seminars called "The Big Book Comes Alive." You can find the entire recordings of these sessions on YouTube, and they are entertaining, educational, and often moving explanations of how AA works.

Joe and Charlie look at the words "our will and our lives" and explain them this way: "Our will" refers to the decisions we make, just as one's last will and testament refers to the decision we make with regard to the final distribution of our property. "Your will" simply means your decisions. "Our will," according to Joe and Charlie, refers to our thinking. "Our lives" refers to the actions we take. The thoughts we've acted upon and the actions we've taken dictate the outcomes of our lives. It's that simple. The new idea of Step Three is that if we invite God to direct our thoughts and our actions, we will end up making better decisions and better choices than if we were left to our own devices.

Sometimes people say in meetings, "My best thinking got me here." In other words, the best idea the speaker had prior to getting sober was to drink to excess for any number of years. That was his best thinking. Now that he has taken Step Three and invited God to direct his thoughts and his actions, he is thinking healthier thoughts, or at least acting upon the healthiest of his thoughts, taking better actions, and therefore getting better results. So Step Three is a blast-off point. It's a moment when the alcoholic leaves her old life behind and allows for a higher power to enter her thinking process and direct it toward better results.

So those are the first three Steps. *I can't. God can. I'm going to let Him.* Or in other words, I have a problem with alcoholism, there's a spiritual solution, and I'm going to avail myself of that spiritual solution. A lot of people in AA try to figure out the difference between "my will" and "God's will." How can a human being possibly tell? AA's response: it's not possible to declare in advance what God's will is. But it's always easy to look back and ask, did I hurt anybody else or myself with my words or my actions? If you did, that's probably not God's will. Wouldn't you agree?

In the early days of AA and, to a small extent, today, members would have "quiet time" first thing in the morning, a few minutes of contemplation, in which they would invite God to speak to them and give them some sense of direction. Some Jews might find this idea strange or even impossible since we believe that prophecy disappeared before the destruction of the Second Temple. There's a difference, however, between a prophet "receiving" the word of God and an AA member receiving messages from his higher power. The prophet's prophecy would affect entire communities, kingdoms, or the whole world. AA members are talking about something much smaller in scope—the idea that God might provide a brief message, a "swing thought" in golf terms, to the individual to act on over the course of that day. You don't have to believe this happens. You don't have to believe anything. AA theology boils down to one simple statement: All you have to know about God is that you aren't God. But if it helps to have some quiet time in the morning with God, then go for it.

Many treatment centers stop after the first three Steps, and even in the meetings, many alcoholics never get further than Step Three. But this is not good enough. So we'll move into the next set of Steps, Four through Seven, which we identified earlier as a process of self-examination. In the early days of Alcoholics Anonymous, you could not even enter a meeting room until you had taken the first three Steps with a sober member, typically in an upstairs bedroom before you were admitted to a meeting in the living room below. A new member would literally get on his knees with the "old-timer" in that upstairs bedroom, turn his will and his life over to God, and then and only then could he get into the meeting room. Things may change, but for the sake of this book, we're going back to basics.

Step 4: Made a searching and fearless moral inventory of ourselves.

Now we get to Step Four: *Made a searching and fearless moral inventory of ourselves.*

When we get here, we don't always like what we see. This may be the first time in our adult lives when we begin to buy into the idea that we might be the problem and not just other people. So if we're going to do any self-examination, we don't want to do it alone. We already want to have a spiritual foundation in place, and we get that spiritual foundation by taking the first three Steps.

Let's look at the language Bill uses in the *Big Book* to describe the purpose of Step Four. Bill was a businessman, so he borrowed the term "inventory" from the business world. Ever go to a store and see a sign that says, "Closed for inventory?" It means that the doors are locked, and the employees are inside, counting all the stuff on the shelves.

Bill carries on the metaphor by speaking of "unsaleable goods." In other words, we're taking a look at ourselves and asking, on the "shelf" of our mind, body, and spirit, what goods are still saleable, and which ones have passed their "use by" date? It's clever, this mercantile approach to understanding ourselves.

Here's another way to understand Step Four: Go tell a kid to clean his room. The likeliest outcome? Stuff will get slightly rearranged if you're lucky. But will it be clean? Of course not. Instead, tell the same kid, "Go to your room and take out all the broken toys, all the toys that are missing pieces, and all the toys that are no fun to play with, and stack them outside your door, to make room for better toys." We both know that in twenty minutes, that room will be spotless.

So another way to think about Step Four is that it is the process by which we identify the broken toys we don't want to play with anymore. For most addicts and alcoholics, those broken toys include anger, fear, resentment, self-pity, manipulation, control, giving away power to others, and other forms of maladaptive behavior.

Could you imagine a life where you are not dominated by these habits of thought and action? It doesn't mean we never slip into these behaviors from time to time. But it means that we aren't stuck in them, living our lives in them, driving ourselves and other people mad, wrecking our lives and theirs, because we continue to behave so badly. That's all the fourth Step is—a process of identifying those broken toys so that we can get rid of them and get better toys to play with. There's also a spiritual reason for focusing on our character defects. It's pretty simple—they block us from continued spiritual growth.

To get into the meat of this Step, I want to go through some of the key "unsaleable goods" that you find in most alcoholics, and which it is the purpose of this Step to remove.

Resentment

Let's begin with resentment, which clearly tops the list. The word "resentment" can be understood as re-sentiment; in other words, feeling a feeling again, and usually in a negative way. Alcoholics and addicts constantly relive past misfortunes. They are big on rehashing past arguments, frustrations, disappointments, failures, bankruptcies, conflicts with law enforcement, and conflicts in general. We do this so much that we say a "balanced alcoholic" is one with a chip on each shoulder.

But it's awfully hard to be comfortable for right now, in the moment, if we are trapped in an endless cycle of resenting people, places, and things. The more we resent, the less we trust. After all, when we are constantly reviewing the history of our interactions with others, if all we see is how they failed us, why should we trust the next person? As a result, we don't trust relatives, friends, employers, or, for that matter, ourselves.

If we have a particularly hard time with a parent, for any reason, it's awfully hard for us to trust any form of authority. So instead of living our lives and maximizing the value of a given day, we find ourselves, day by day, sinking further and further into the mire of distrust, disappointment, and frustration. Identifying and releasing, to another human being and to God, our resentments is a way to free ourselves from the pain they cause. Doing so allows us to live in the moment, which is the only place where God can be found.

Fear

After releasing resentment, the next common topic of the fourth Step is fear. In the *Big Book*, Bill W. tells us there are "a thousand forms of fear," but he doesn't specify what each of the thousand forms is. Instead, he focuses on one type, which he calls "self-centered fear."

Bill describes self-centered fear as "the fear of not getting what you want or the fear of losing what you have." This is the core fear that dominates the thinking of virtually every practicing addict and alcoholic. Our world gets smaller and smaller as we run out of resources, friends, jobs, places to stay, and other necessities of life. Since we are on a losing streak of massive proportions, it stands to reason that we will fear losing what little else we have.

And then at the same time, when we start thinking about what we want to get, or what we hope we might get, instead we find ourselves in fear that even if we get it, we will lose it. Once again, we are prisoners of our emotions, stuck in the never-ending rat trap of trying to hang on to what little we have, while at the same time being concerned that we will never attain anything more.

Fear, by itself, isn't a bad thing. Sometimes it's appropriate. But fear crosses a line from useful to destructive when it inhibits or even cripples our ability to function appropriately. Little in life is enhanced by overwhelming fear. And yet, as alcoholics and addicts who just keep on losing, it's natural to fear that our losses will continue to mount.

Anger

After resentment and fear comes anger. The *Big Book* speaks of anger as a "corrosive thread" in our lives, and it's hard to disagree with that assessment. Anger in and of itself is not bad. It's a God-given instinct, and psychologists tell us that anger actually indicates a desire for change. The trouble is that alcoholics take anger a little too far.

First, as the expression goes, alcoholics and addicts don't *get* angry. They *are* angry. Anger and rebelliousness are a natural state of mind for the practicing addict or alcoholic.

Paradoxically, the emotion is both comforting and upsetting. Anger makes the practicing addict or alcoholic feel powerful. Most of the time, he feels impotent, and if he can work himself into a good rage, the adrenalin flows and he is unstoppable. When we're angry, everything is everybody else's fault. We don't have to look at our part in anything, nor would we want to.

At the same time, overwhelming anger, which is pretty much the only kind that alcoholics know, is just too much to contain. The expression "going nuclear" fits nicely. Anger creates so much energy inside us that we can't keep it within. We find ourselves exploding—at ourselves, at others, at loved ones, at strangers, at the police, at prison guards, and whoever happens to have the misfortune of being in our way.

In 1966, Truman Capote wrote one of the first "nonfiction novels" about two young men from a town called Pleasant, Kansas, who seemingly randomly killed a family. When the police tried to learn why they had done it, the answer was that they had been abused as children, and "somebody has to pay for it." That's the trouble with anger. If something bad happened to me, then somebody has to pay for it. The alcoholic or addict is desirous of only one thing—to not be the one who pays the price. Someone else will.

That's why the *Big Book* talks about how destruction can fall upon blameless children, furniture, or whatever or whoever is at hand. By contrast, a little internal anger isn't a bad thing. It's just our way of indicating to ourselves that we want to change. The problem comes when we aren't able to contain it and we find ourselves lashing out, inevitably with bad results. Is it possible to have this corrosive thread—the inappropriate experience of anger, and the inappropriate direction of anger toward others, removed from our lives? Absolutely.

Control

So far, we've talked about resentment, fear, and anger. Here's one more character defect that plagues alcoholics: the urge to compulsively control others. Practicing addicts and alcoholics feel out of control, so their natural response is to seek to over-control everyone and everything in sight.

The *Big Book* addresses this very point, about how alcoholics like to be the director of the play, doing the choreography, the lights, and everything else. In real life, alcoholics are constantly handing other people scripts, dictating what they should say, do, and feel, and woe to any of them who do not follow their orders to the letter.

If you had a childhood where you never knew whether the parent approaching the house would be Dr. Jekyll or Mr. Hyde if your parents' personalities were so mercurial that they could change at the drop of a hat, if you weren't sure that the rent and bills would be paid unless you paid them yourself, and you were nine years old, doing what the adult should have been doing, and so on, there's a very good chance that you'd come into your adult life desperate for control. For the typical alcoholic, control isn't just a hobby or a whim. It's a survival mechanism. The problem is that most people don't like being controlled. They don't like being told, over and over again, what to do.

Bill repeatedly explains in AA's book known as the *12 and 12* that when a person has a healthy relationship with his higher power, he no longer needs to play God to his fellows or allow them to play God to him. In other words, in recovery, people reach a point where they are able to finally live and let live—to allow the people around them to go on with their lives, be who they are meant to be, and enjoy themselves, without making them crazy every step of the way. If you think your relationships are enhanced by your need to compulsively over-control everyone around you, then you may not want to give up this defect of character just yet. But if you trying to control others alienates them, then maybe addressing the character defect of being controlling will pay off for you.

Step 5: Admitted to God, to ourselves, and to another human being the exact nature of our wrongs.

The fourth and fifth Steps are conjoined. The fourth Step is where you write your inventory or have your sponsor write it for you. The fifth Step is where you share all of that with your sponsor or some other trusted person. Here's the actual language of the Step: *Admitted to God, to ourselves, and to another human being the exact nature of our wrongs.*

Whether you do the writing by yourself, or you and your sponsor get together to do it, the fifth Step is all about the recognition that "we are only as sick as our secrets." It's healthy to tell the truth as best as we can about ourselves. It only goes so far if we are just telling these truths to ourselves. It's so much more powerful and soul-shaping if we share these uncomfortable realizations with another person, someone we trust.

The *Big Book* asks us to be careful as we make a choice of who to write and share our inventories with. It might be a sponsor or a religious leader. The *Big Book* shies away from us using an individual with whom we are emotionally bound, such as a partner or spouse, because such a person may not need to know everything that a fourth and fifth Step entail. If there's no one in the program with whom you're comfortable enough to do a fourth and fifth Steps, the book suggests that we find a clergyman or clergywoman, or a trusted professional such as a therapist or psychiatrist.

Alcoholics who haven't someone to trust in the AA fellowship with their fourth Step probably haven't been looking hard enough. There's always someone, and if you just give yourself a chance to get to know people, you will almost certainly find someone to whom you feel comfortable opening up. Ultimately, what matters most is that you actually get this conversation done. It's a chance to acknowledge, out loud, to another person and to your higher power, the fact that we are human. Instead of lying, evading, denying, and lawyering up, we're finally telling the truth about ourselves.

So that's why we include another person and our higher power in this conversation. If we just tell these things to ourselves, that's a positive step, after all the lying to ourselves that we have most likely done over the decades. But if we tell another person, that's even better, because we have taken a major step toward getting honest, which is essential if addicts and alcoholics are going to live in recovery. But best of all, we are telling our higher power, because we are taking a step—admittedly, an uncomfortable step—toward freedom. And isn't that what recovery is all about?

Step 6: We are entirely ready to have God remove all these defects of character.

Now comes Step Six: *We are entirely ready to have God remove all these defects of character.* Step Six is about recognizing that every character defect has a *benefit*. If I'm angry, I feel powerful. If I'm fearful, I don't have to do what I don't want to do, whether it's going to work, paying my bills, or even doing the laundry. I was too afraid, so I didn't do it. If I'm controlling, I feel more secure. If I'm envious, I can assure myself that you are a bad person and that you don't deserve what you have.

If I'm resentful, I'm living in the past. If I'm projecting, I'm living in the future. Either way, I don't have to focus on what a mess my life is today. In other words, when I'm practicing one of my character defects, I'm actually getting some sort of payoff from it. So the real Step Six question is this: Am I entirely ready, or even partially ready, to give up the benefits of each of my defects of character? As the expression goes, it's never too late to be the person you were always meant to be.

Step 7: Humbly asked Him to remove our shortcomings.

Step Seven is where we complete the process we began in Step Four, where we identified the defects of character and now we are going to ask our higher power to remove them. The humility of this Step is not about being struck with the "nice person" wand and suddenly going from prideful to humble overnight.

Instead, Step Seven is where you indicate to yourself, to your sponsor, and to your higher power that you want to live differently, and that you want to be a better person.

At this point, your sponsor will list the character defects you've identified in this process, and then will ask you this question: "Just for today, would you be willing to give these defects of character to the God of your understanding?"

So now the beginning of a process that lasts a lifetime— the willingness to acknowledge our shortcomings, and the commitment to do the right thing instead of the wrong thing wherever possible. Just because you *ask* your higher power to remove all your defects of character doesn't mean it will happen overnight. Change takes time. Be patient with yourself. You will get there.

Next, come Steps Eight and Nine, the amends Steps:

Step 8: Made a list of all persons we had harmed and became willing to make amends to them all.

Bill divided the process of making amends or fixing broken relationships, into two phases. The first is about identifying people or institutions we have harmed or to whom we owe an apology or monetary recompense. These can include family members, people we've dated, employers, businesses, or even the IRS. The operative word is "harm"—people in recovery only make amends, or sincere statements of apology, to those whose lives (or finances) were negatively affected by the alcoholic's behavior. No harm, no amend.

The process is sometimes described as "cleaning up one's side of the street." In other words, we don't take into account what the other person did or said to provoke our bad behavior. We just look at what *we* did or said. If our actions caused harm, the name goes on the list.

Step 9: Made direct amends to such people wherever possible, except when to do so would injure them or others.

When recovering alcoholics and addicts think about making amends, all they think about is how miserable it's going to be to have to go back to the people they hurt and say they're sorry. Yet it actually feels *awesome* to see the look in the eyes of someone you hurt badly who is actually happy with you instead of still wanting to kill you. It's not like anything you've ever seen before in your life. It's a combination of respect, empathy, and even admiration. They may not rehire you or get back into a relationship with you. But you will see in *their* eyes the fact that you are a changed person.

You cannot un-ring the bell. You cannot go back in time and undo the thing you did. But you can go back to the person you harmed and transform the relationship, even if you never see each other again.

There are two ways to think of amends. One is that you are mending—you are fixing—broken relationships. The other is that you are repaying a debt. When we think about money, it's pretty obvious. If you borrowed or stole money, you owe the money. Just as with money, we steal other things from people. We steal time. We steal affection. So an amend is a means of paying back a debt that we have incurred, whether it is financial, spiritual, or any other kind.

When people first get into recovery, the last thing they want to do is think about making amends. They're still too busy thinking about all the ways in which the world has harmed them.

And then once they start going through the Steps, they can still feel pretty resentful toward people with whom they got into various forms of scrapes. So it makes sense that they're not going to become all that thrilled about making amends to everyone the moment they start the Steps. Nobody hit them with that "good guy" stick and they didn't go from imperfect to perfect overnight, so they understand that it will take a little longer to make certain amends.

Once they get around to making them, they can do the easy ones first. There's no special rule about the order in which amends are made. Right now, all the Steps ask you to do is to open your mind to the idea that everybody who deserves an amend will eventually get one from you, and the sooner the better. You just start on your list and keep going.

How soon after you've completed Step Eight should you start making amends? Once you've gone over your list with your sponsor, get going. There's a famous story in AA that Dr. Bob, our Akron cofounder, disappeared for a day shortly after he had gotten sober. Everybody thought he was dead drunk again. In reality, he was just out there making his amends to all the folks who deserved one. He didn't get back until after midnight, but when he did, he was extremely happy. Mission accomplished.

Making amends is a vital part of the recovery program in Alcoholics Anonymous and all other twelve-step programs. It's not likely that we're going to enjoy the benefits of long-term, contented sobriety if we fail to make the amends we owe.

Step 10: Continued to take personal inventory and when we were wrong promptly admitted it.

The short course on Step Ten is that it's about continuing to monitor your behavior and continuing to make amends "when we were wrong"—not if, but when. Why? Because recovery is not a game of perfect. You will continue to do and say the wrong things. Not as often, and the repercussions typically won't be as drastic. You get to be happier, better people. The level of anger within diminishes with time, conscious application of the Steps, and full participation in our twelve-step fellowship, as a member, as a sponsor and a sponsee (they call it the "sponsor sandwich"), and through random (and sustained) acts of service. But you will still stumble in your relationships with yourself and with others. This Step teaches that instead of letting the mistakes pile up, we admit to them and make our amends right away.

Step 11: Sought through prayer and meditation to improve our conscious contact with God as we understood Him, praying only for knowledge of His will for us and the power to carry that out.

Now we circle back to the relationship with our higher power that we began to develop in Steps Two and Three. We come to see how important prayer and meditation (to be more precise, contemplation of our higher power) really are.

Step 12: Having had a spiritual awakening as the result of these Steps, we tried to carry this message to alcoholics, and to practice these principles in all our affairs.

We now see that our spirits have reawakened, and we carry the message of recovery to sick and suffering alcoholics and addicts, in and out of the rooms. If people at work know that you are clean and sober, it is not ideal to be stealing office supplies, doing less than your fair share, or practicing office politics when you should be doing your job.

We are carrying a message about twelve-step recovery all the time, even when we are not talking about the program or doing program-related things. Remember that your alcoholic and addicted friends, coworkers, relatives, and neighbors are watching you carefully to see if twelve-step recovery is real. It is very real, and the emphasis on character development that we discussed in Steps Four through Nine is vital to stay sober and be good examples of the fellowship for everyone else to witness.

***

Twelve-step recovery is about attraction, not promotion. We can't "sell" the program to other people. All anyone can do is model the benefits it has, in terms of removing alcoholics from the grips of addiction and restoring them to their place in society.

In the next chapter, we will look more closely at how we Jews can support families and friends struggling within our community. Making the effort to understand the twelve steps is a powerful first step. Let's take the next step by exploring what early sobriety looks like and the power of Al-Anon.

CHAPTER 10

Understanding Early Sobriety

A s we learn to set aside the stigma against the alcoholics and addicts among us, we start to ask, "So what can we do to help?"

Good news, bad news. Let's start with the bad news. You can't *change* the alcoholic or addict in your family or community, and you can't force him or her to stop drinking or using. So you can let go of that idea right now. Your expectations, timetable, list of grievances, and judgment are best left at the door.

The good news is you can *influence* the addict or alcoholic you know, and be either a source that supports and enables the person to seek recovery or prevents and impedes it. So in the spirit of knowing the difference between what we can and cannot change, let's jump into what you *can* do that will help the addict in your life.

What Is Early Sobriety?

The first thing we can do is *learn more about addiction and recovery*. And part of learning about addiction and recovery is understanding what early sobriety looks like.

What does it mean to live in recovery? On a day-to-day basis, what is the experience of the recovering alcoholic or addict? And what can loved ones expect in what time frame? While the experience of every recovering person is different, and we cannot put precise timelines on when various personal, spiritual, or professional milestones may be reached, we can certainly discuss, in a general way, the "what now" for people in recovery and their families.

Deciding to Seek Treatment

Your first question may be, *When will this person decide to seek treatment?* I wish I had a crystal ball that could offer that prediction. Ultimately, no one can say because, for some addicts, the answer may be never. In general, addicts stop acting out when the pain of continuing to do so, in their minds, outweighs the pain of letting go of the addiction. The addict might want to stop his addictive behavior patterns, but let's face it: He likes getting high. He likes the thrill of doing naughty things. And if he's far enough along in his addiction, willpower can't curtail his behavior.

Which is why sometimes it takes the proverbial "gun in the mouth" moment for an addict or alcoholic to decide, *that's it, I've got to stop.* They experience some consequence to their drinking, using, or acting out, some crisis, that can no longer be comfortably—or uncomfortably—ignored. This might come in the form of an ultimatum from a spouse. A humiliating public scene. A car accident. An arrest. Suicidal thoughts. Whatever it is, let's put it this way: *Most people don't come into twelve-step recovery on a winning streak.* Instead, they have to lose and lose and lose, and then lose some more, before they realize that the game is truly over and stopping is the only sensible act.

Sometimes that moment of truth comes about because family and friends organize what's called an "intervention," a meeting in which friends and family members will gather together to tell the addict or alcoholic how their behavior has affected them. Interventions are typically organized by professionals who specialize in the production of such gatherings. Everyone present will either speak about how the addictive behavior of the individual has hurt them or betrayed them. Some interventionists have attendees write letters that they read at the event so that their emotions don't cause them to forget key points. At the end of the intervention, the alcoholic or addict is invited to enter treatment, and arrangements have usually been made in advance, typically by the interventionist, for a bed in a recovery facility focused on the specific issue or issues the individual presents.

But let's not get too optimistic here. Some people have been to a dozen or more such facilities before they overdose and die or before their families stop throwing money at their recovery. Interventions are not everyday occurrences. Some people have sat through interventions, gone off to rehab, and never drank or used again. For others, the intervention had no effect whatsoever. When it comes to addiction, there are no guarantees. But not every person starting off recovery needs to go through an intervention or go to a treatment center. Plenty of alcoholics and addicts of all stripes pick themselves up and simply go to twelve-step meetings, get into therapy, or find some other approach to quitting.

A Bumpy Ride

Once an addict or alcoholic *does* decide to seek or agree to treatment, the ride can be a bit bumpy. In other words, there is some backsliding in the recovery process. Often, an addict goes through a few false starts, getting a few days or weeks away from the behavior or substance, slipping and going back to it, getting some more clean time, and then finally getting the plane into the air. The relevant twelve-step cliché is that "a slip is not a fall." In other words, brief periods of relapse may happen, but don't panic. Letting go of a lifetime of compulsive behavior doesn't always happen on the timetable of the addict or their family. Patience is the order of the day.

Some people will never drink or use again after their first contact with twelve-step recovery. Others will dance with their disease, trying to moderate their use of drugs, alcohol, or other substances and behaviors, only to discover the sorry truth that alcoholics and addicts don't taper off, they taper *on*. Which is why total abstinence is the only total solution.

Consistency, Sponsors, and Taking the Steps

Early in recovery, newcomers are given the suggestion to go to meetings on days ending with the letter "y," or to go to meetings on the days of the week they would have drank or used (that's every day of the week). In other words, to succeed in recovery, the addict needs to put as much time and effort into going to meetings as she did when she was trying to find her alcohol, drugs, bookie, or what have you. Consistency is key. Many addicts stumble in recovery not because they couldn't succeed, but because they stopped going to meetings and stopped working the steps.

Sponsors are individuals who have been in recovery, and who work one-on-one with another person in recovery. They explain how to make a success of oneself in twelve-step recovery and answer questions the newcomer may have about living without one's addictive substances and behaviors. Sponsors will also guide the newcomer through the Twelve Steps. The language of the Steps is somewhat convoluted. Though not impossible, it is difficult to take them by oneself. This is why twelve-step programs use the sponsorship model.

Relief comes from meetings. If you go to a meeting, you'll feel better. Meetings are essential for recovery, even for those who've been clean, sober, and abstinent for decades. You never stop going to meetings. You may go to three or four meetings a week instead of seven or nine, but you keep going. Recovery, however, comes from taking the Steps. Taking the Steps creates the insurance policy against relapse that allows the newcomer to move into a position of certainty that as long as they continue to do what they're asked to do—clean house, trust God, help others—they won't find it necessary to drink or use, a day at a time, forever.

Love-Hate

Some addicts and alcoholics love twelve-step meetings from the first moment. They're so happy to meet other people who understand them and aren't judging them. They're thrilled to find a way out of a life that has become increasingly miserable, cramped, and lonely. They've either tried to commit suicide or the thought has passed their minds. If I may generalize, many alcoholics and addicts know exactly how they would kill themselves. Non-alcoholics seldom make such plans.

Other newcomers to recovery literally grieve the fact that they have to go to meetings, that the game is over, and that they have lost their best, most trusted friend. Addicts trust their substances far more than they trust their loved ones. People can say "no," but booze, drugs, gambling bets, and the like always say "yes." So there's a surprising period of mourning that accompanies early sobriety. If you lost your best, most trusted friend, you'd mourn, too. The important thing here is not to judge the addict in your life because of this mourning period. It's normal.

Celebrating Successes

In many twelve-step meetings, newcomers are invited to "count days." This means that they are invited to announce their name, the nature of their disease, and how many days clean they have, as in, "My name is Joe and I'm an alcoholic, and today is day fifty-three." Or, "I'm Mary, I'm a gambling addict, and I have ninety days today."

In many meetings, each such announcement is greeted with a round of applause. There's something addictive, in a positive way, about being acknowledged for handling a situation that was always so shameful. So "counting days" is often a successful way to draw newcomers back to meetings.

Over the course of the first year in recovery, the primary goal...is simply to complete the first year of recovery. Pretty much all addicts and alcoholics come to twelve-step programs hoping that by the end of their first year clean and sober, they will have attained a complete recovery of their reputations, marriages, families, careers, and fortunes. Or if they've never had any of those things, they expect that since they've been good boys and girls and have stopped acting out, they are entitled to all sorts of cash and prizes.

By the time they've reached their first-year anniversary, which is a big celebration, they've come to the somewhat humbling realization that though they've made a beginning at rebuilding their lives, this process is going to take a minute longer than they might have expected. Still, the first year anniversary is a great cause for celebration. Newcomers are asked to keep track of the date of the last time they engaged in their addictive behavior, for the simple reason that if they cannot remember when their last drink or drug use took place, they probably haven't had it yet. Declaring a sobriety date is like drawing a line in the sand of time. It's saying, "I'm going to defend this date with everything I've got. I'm going to do everything I can so that a year from that date, I can be honored at my meetings for reaching this enormous milestone."

It's not always an enormous milestone for loved ones, who may not realize how hard it is for addicts to stop and stay stopped. I know a very successful attorney in his fifties who told his mother that he hadn't had any alcohol or drugs for two years. Unimpressed, his mother growled, "Neither has the cat." Maybe that's why he drank.

You may be invited to give your recovering family member a year coin or candle or other mementos at a meeting. If you're asked, consider it an honor, and go. You may get a chance to say a few words about your loved one, depending on the meeting's format. It's not a roast. It's not an opportunity to lay blame. It's a happy day, so keep it that way. Keep your remarks brief, positive, and oriented toward gratitude. And why not? Your loved one has achieved the seemingly impossible: He or she has regained the power of choice by embracing a deeper spiritual life.

That's a big deal.

Changes to Expect

At some point, your loved one may approach you to "make amends," to apologize for what he or she has done, as described in the previous chapter. Addicts and alcoholics are given the suggestion—not the requirement—to make amends to those they have harmed. They typically make those amends or have those conversations only after they've taken the prior Steps with their sponsor and have discussed thoroughly the conversations they're about to have with you and others. The conversation may ring hollow to you, or perhaps you will perceive that your loved one is being sincere. Don't judge. Just say thank you.

Sometimes newcomers take "sobriety jobs"—temping or working as a barista or delivering packages, something to demonstrate to themselves and others that their time is worthwhile and that they can be useful and reliable to other people. Once they've got a little bit of time under their belt, it makes sense for them to complete their education, return to their normal career, or otherwise make a go of life once again.

If you feel antsy about your loved one's progress, and want them to jump back into more substantial work or life involvement, it's important to remember that there is no specific timetable that can be applied to emotional and spiritual growth. If the recovering person in your life is attending meetings regularly, taking the Steps, and being sponsored, for the time being, you really can't ask for more.

Compassion Goes a Long Way

Sometimes you may recognize the positive changes that alcoholics and addicts make in their lives before they themselves do. The recovering person may not be aware that he or she is doing things better than before. When you do notice, a little bit of encouragement goes a long way. Does this mean that you have to take the person back into your home, cancel the divorce proceedings, rehire him or her, or otherwise resume cordial relations as before? Well, they probably weren't that cordial, certainly at the end. But the answer is no. You don't have to do anything you don't want to do.

All one can do is plead for compassion and understanding, which will be enhanced if you attend some meetings with the recovering person in your life and if you give Al-Anon or any of its sister programs a try. Support and encouragement, when not overbearing or manipulative, may mean the world to the recovering person, who is unquestionably struggling to regain a sense of sanity and control. Do what you can to provide it.

Humbled by the Power of AA

As people watch their loved ones walk the path of recovery through AA or another program, they may have different reactions. For some, it's gratifying that twelve-step programs exist with the sole purpose of helping people like your loved one escape from addiction, once and for all, a day at a time. For others who might have been trying to get their loved one clean and sober over a period of months or years, the feeling is different. It's frustrating when a bunch of backslapping strangers in a church basement are able to accomplish, sometimes seemingly overnight, what they were not able to accomplish in all that time.

"I was saying the same thing they're saying in the meetings!" these folks exclaim. Well, sometimes your loved one has to hear it from a stranger. The stranger is the person with whom your loved one has no history. There's no baggage. There are no expectations. There's no guilt.

Instead of feeling one-upped, let the twelve-step programs work their magic. Get over yourself and be glad that someone got your loved one sober, even if you didn't manage that feat. And be patient. Stopping drinking or using doesn't immediately change the addict's personality. That takes time, meetings, and the Steps.

In the next chapter, we're going to look at a program designed for family and friends of addicts and alcoholics, Al-Anon. Though this chapter should have given you a taste of what you can expect and how you can support your loved one, Al-Anon is without question the most powerful resource for people with alcoholics or addicts in their lives.

CHAPTER 11

The Life-Changing Power of Al-Anon

You have an addict or alcoholic in your life. What now? What can you do? What can you *not* do?

This was the question that Lois Wilson, the long-suffering wife of Alcoholics Anonymous co-founder Bill Wilson, faced. No doubt she was delighted when Bill got sober. It was the answer to a prayer of many years standing for her (and her entire family). The only problem was that Bill, unfortunately, found a lot more satisfaction in his role as leader of AA than he did as the husband of Lois Wilson. In fact, his record as a husband leaves a lot to be desired. At one point, he had become so neglectful of Lois that she actually took off her shoe and threw it at him, saying, "Damn your old meetings."

At that moment, Lois realized that she needed help as well because years of living with a practicing alcoholic had exacted a huge toll on her own mental health. And thus, with the help of a friend, she created what today is known as Al-Anon Family Groups or Al-Anon for short. The core idea of Al-Anon is that loved ones, friends, and coworkers of alcoholics and addicts suffer enormously, grievously, and behind closed doors. No one understands the suffering of the spouse or the parent of an alcoholic or addict.

Well-meaning friends and even rabbis give advice that isn't always grounded in reality—throw them out, take them back, bail them out of jail, let them sit in jail for a couple of nights. The advice is often contradictory and often ineffective or even destructive. So the question becomes how can a loved one of an alcoholic or addict find support and practical, proven guidance while going through the brutally painful experience of enduring the addictive behavior of the addict?

That's the question that Al-Anon answers for its members. To combat the isolation, Al-Anon has meetings just like AA meetings. They're usually smaller, but the format is practically identical. These meetings allow relatives and friends of alcoholics to recognize that other people are suffering the same way they are suffering, and that other people have found it possible to live contented lives whether the alcoholic is still drinking or using or not. The message of Al-Anon family groups: There's hope and there's help for you, whether the alcoholic or addict in your life stops using or not.

What Our Addicts Do to Us

Before getting into the details of how Al-Anon can help, I'd like to share a shocking truth that Al-Anon teaches: *Close contact with an alcoholic or addict warps the personality of loved ones to the point where they actually develop the same personality traits as the alcoholic or addict, minus the need to drink or use.*

This is such a shocking statement that it bears reiterating: Family members of alcoholics or addicts take on the same negative personality traits as their alcoholic or addicted relatives, minus the compulsion to drink or use.

How can this be?

First, let's consider what happens to us when we have an alcoholic or addict in our lives. Parents may have it the worst. The guilt that parents feel over having an addicted child, whether the child is twelve years old or middle-aged, can barely be described. It's so painful because parents usually feel responsible for the choices their children make. "If I had been a better mother…" "If I hadn't been such a tough father…" and so on.

Spouses torture themselves as well, asking, "What was I thinking, marrying a drunk?" Or "If he doesn't quit by New Year's, should I leave?" Or, "Why couldn't I see the signs before we got married and had kids?" To be married to an addict or alcoholic is a humiliating, miserable, thankless experience. The same kind of persistent feelings of pain, inadequacy, and guilt that often fuel the addict's behavior starts to take root in those living with or around the addict as well. A pervasive sense of suffering takes hold. The need to conceal the loved one's secret leads to lying—to oneself and others.

Since that's the case, it makes sense that the same Twelve Steps that help an addict or alcoholic stop using and stay stopped would also help the family member of the alcoholic or addict to achieve a state of happiness and serenity, whether the alcoholic is still drinking or not. This is why, in Al-Anon, members take the same Steps that alcoholics take in AA and addicts take in Cocaine Anonymous, Narcotics Anonymous, Marijuana Anonymous, Psychedelics Anonymous, and so on. In fact, the Twelve Steps as used in Al-Anon modify only one word. In the twelfth Step, where it says in the AA version, "we carry this message to alcoholics," the Al-Anon version reads, "we carry this message to others."

Just as the addict's recovery is dependent on her willingness to share what she has found with others, so the recovery of the person in Al-Anon depends on that person's willingness to share what she has gained in Al-Anon with other individuals who are related to, married to, or otherwise closely involved with addicts or alcoholics.

What to Expect from Al-Anon

What can you expect when you attend an Al-Anon meeting for the first time? Pretty much the same thing as when you attend an AA meeting, or any other twelve-step meeting, for that matter. You'll find the same sense of order, calm, and structure. After introductions and readings from Al-Anon literature, typically including a reading of the Twelve Steps, members will speak about a given topic, a piece of literature, or a slogan that encapsulates the Al-Anon way of life. Actually, most Al-Anon slogans are the same as those found in AA meeting rooms—Turn It Over, Live and Let Live, Take It Easy, and Think. The Think sign will almost certainly be upside-down. It's okay. It's supposed to be upside-down. The idea is that our thinking is limited but God's thinking is unlimited, so we "turn over" to God the challenges and frustrations we experience. His plan is inevitably better than ours.

Members will speak from two to five minutes, with someone keeping time on his or her phone.[23] Time to speak is set aside for newcomers at most Al-Anon meetings, but as in AA, there is no obligation to speak or even identify yourself by name. That's actually one slight difference—in an AA meeting, people will identify themselves by first name and the phrase, "I'm an alcoholic," while in Al-Anon, it's first names only. Why just first names? Two reasons. First and last names tend to identify people with ethnicity and sometimes religion. In twelve-step groups, the focus is on what binds people together, not what separates them. Second, Anonymous programs are meant to be…anonymous. Surprise?

In Al-Anon, people typically also do not use the name of the alcoholic whose problem drinking caused them to come to the fellowship in the first place. Instead, people will talk about their "qualifier," the individual whose behavior qualifies them to come to Al-Anon. So if you hear the word "qualifier," now you know what that means. They will often identify the person by family relationship, as in my husband, my son, my wife, etc. Protecting the anonymity of the alcoholic is fundamental in Al-Anon.

At this point, you might be saying, what are they going to tell me in Al-Anon that I don't already know? My Shloimie is a drunk. Now what?

Fortunately, the answer is plenty.

---

23   Otherwise the program wouldn't be Al-Anon—it would be OnAndOn.

Ten Benefits of Al-Anon

I thought I might share with you ten benefits of coming to Al-Anon, by which I mean not just dropping in once or twice but actually taking part on a regular basis, committing to attending meetings regularly, getting and using a sponsor, taking the Steps, reading the literature, and so on. Think of it as a graduate seminar in "How to understand, love, and actually help the problem drinker in your life." So here we go.

1. *Acceptance.*

Acceptance of a situation is a cornerstone of any twelve-step program. Acceptance doesn't mean liking something or weak-kneed submission to a dangerous or despicable situation. In fact, Al-Anon counsels that if there is physical violence in the home, take your kids and get out.

Rather, acceptance in Al-Anon means *accepting the facts of a situation.* In other words, it means accepting the *reality* of having an alcoholic spouse, child, or partner and making the best of things. It means getting out of denial about the fact that one's daughter, husband, parent, or whoever is a problem drinker. As long as I'm denying the reality of a situation, I cannot begin to solve the problem for myself or others. In essence, I'm lying to myself out of a sense of misguided hope that the problem will somehow solve itself. It seldom does.

This was the bias when Al-Anon was founded in the 1940s, and it's still the case. In the Orthodox world, where divorce is usually the least desirable option, the Al-Anon bias is similar: Make the best of things without destroying the marriage.

Acceptance isn't easy, but it's necessary if the loved one of an alcoholic is going to have peace of mind or any form of sanity. Recovery begins with accepting the reality of a situation so that appropriate steps can be taken. Al-Anon counsels acceptance.

2. Getting off the "merry-go-round of denial."

As we saw earlier, sometimes alcoholics and addicts like to goad loved ones into arguments so they can go sulk, have a pity party, and justify themselves by getting drunk, getting high, or acting out in an addictive manner with any of the other substances or behaviors we've discussed. Al-Anon teaches its members to identify when the alcoholic or addict is engaging in such argument-seeking behavior. It really does take two to tango.

If you are not willing to resume your normal role of argument partner, if you stop trying to harass the alcoholic or addict into giving up inappropriate substances or behaviors, the alcoholic or addict feels very much alone. You've taken a lot of the pleasure out of his drinking and using. Sometimes, simply getting off that merry-go-round is sufficient to move the alcoholic to seek treatment. It doesn't happen every time, but it happens a lot.

3. Verbal jiu-jitsu.

Typically, those who love alcoholics and addicts are so burned out by the behavior of their loved ones that their conversational strategies are all about arguing, anger, and contempt. They feel justified in speaking angrily, even furiously, because of all the bad behavior to which the addict or alcoholic is subjecting him or her. But do you really feel good about yourself when you argue, yell, or seek to humiliate your loved one? What message are the kids getting from you? Are you portraying yourself as a victim? You may well feel victimized, but are you essentially training your kids to see you as a victim and seeing yourself as a victim as well? What if there was another way to enter into dialogue with an alcoholic who wants to argue so as not to justify another spree?

Al-Anon teaches its members not to engage or argue because engagement and argument are pointless. Al-Anon suggests using phrases like, "You might be right," even when the alcoholic says the most ridiculous thing in the world, or "Hmm." How can the alcoholic or addict argue with "Hmm?" In other words, by choosing not to engage in pointless verbal jousting, you protect your own dignity and save yourself from yet another round of fruitless bickering, which tears at your own soul and doesn't do the kids any good, either.

Al-Anon also advises putting yourself into the "Al-Anon bubble," an invisible protective sphere in which you imagine yourself comfortably encased. When you're in the Al-Anon bubble, the angry words, the criticism, and the meanness (pretty much all of which is self-hatred directed outward) bounces off the bubble and cannot reach you. In extreme cases, Al-Anon even suggests that you imagine the alcoholic standing on the second floor of a mental hospital with his robe open, saying those same things. It's harder to take all that negativity seriously if he's standing on the balcony of a mental institution with his robe open, wouldn't you agree? The point is not to match humiliation with humiliation. The point is to protect you from the anger and rage that alcoholics dish out on others, which hurt you as much as the alcoholic or addict.

4. *Compassion.*

Most people who are closely related to alcoholics and addicts, whether they are parents, children, spouses, or otherwise, feel just burned out by all the bad behavior, the crises, the disappointments, and the lies. Who wouldn't feel that way? The problem is that going through life with such a high level of resentment is injurious to the mental and often physical health of the relative or the spouse of the alcoholic. You often hear people in twelve-step meetings saying that resenting someone else is like taking poison and waiting for the other person to die.

One of the most important and subtle benefits of Al-Anon is the ability to distinguish between the *disease of addiction*, which is nightmarish, and *the person suffering from the disease.* Al-Anon teaches compassion. Would we be angry at a loved one who, God forbid, was diagnosed with cancer or heart disease? Wouldn't we feel compassion for that person? Yes, a person with that sort of diagnosis typically does not engage in the same sort of bad behavior that is the hallmark of addiction. But the question is whether we can recognize that even though she may be dishing out a lot of misery on other people, the addict herself is suffering, too.

Remember that most people who drink to the level of passing out or spend their family savings on cocaine or heroin aren't doing so because they are having a happy day and just want to get happier. They are trying to kill pain, but the methods they choose are dangerous, devastating to loved ones, and often life-threatening. It's a miserable way to go through life.

Al-Anon teaches its members to balance a sense of compassion for the addict with not buying into the addict's lies or justifications for his or her behavior. It's a lot easier to go through life feeling a sense of compassion for a suffering loved one than to feel consumed with hatred and even murderous intent. You might say, "I could never feel forgiving or accepting about my alcoholic spouse or partner." Never say never. A few months in Al-Anon and you may feel very differently.

5. *Connectedness.*

The first time you go to an Al-Anon meeting and you hear people telling parts of your story, it will be one of the most astonishing hours of your life. Most people who love alcoholics and addicts feel as though they are the only ones on the planet going through what they are going through, and that no one else could possibly understand. The sense of identification with others who are also suffering from the effects of an alcoholic marriage, or living with an addicted teenage son or daughter, will come as a huge relief.

You are not alone. You are not the only one. Other people are going through the same thing, and because they are in Al-Anon, not only have they found a way out of their own misery, but they want to help you understand and improve your situation as well. And this is the case whether the alcoholic or addict is still using or not, and whether the alcoholic or addict is still alive or dead, for that matter. This common cause among members of Al-Anon provides a sense of connectedness which goes a long way toward dispelling the loneliness and isolation that most people feel because they love an addict or alcoholic.

Most alcoholic or addicted homes are governed by "no-talk rules." This means that there is a tacit agreement among family members never to discuss with anyone outside the home the realities of what happens inside. "No-talk rules" are foundational in such homes because people are typically so embarrassed and shy about all the negativity and misery that living with an alcoholic entails. What if the neighbors find out? Or the people at our synagogue? It would be humiliating! Sound familiar?

By contrast, in the safe cocoon of an Al-Anon meeting, it's possible for family members to talk openly about the challenges, misery, and dilemmas that living with an addict or alcoholic creates. The sense of connectedness goes a long way toward making life worth living once again for people who have been suffering so brutally from the effects of the disease on their loved ones.

6. *Boundaries.*

In alcoholic or addictive homes, boundaries are fluid. It's hard to see where you end and I begin. You're all up in my business, and I'm all up in your business. There are no limits. There's no privacy. It's a mess. This lack of boundaries mimics the codependent phase that follows the birth of a child and is reiterated in the early stages of new relationships. Let me explain.

In developmental psychology, we learn that when a baby is born, the baby has no concept of self. He does not know where he ends and the mother begins. There is a sense of oneness and connectedness, which is appropriate at that stage of development. Similarly, in the earliest stages of a relationship, typically the first three or four months, there is an absolutely oceanic feeling of deep, even complete connection to the other person. You feel fused to the beloved.

You cannot wait to speak to him or her again. Conversations go on and on for hours. You feel as though you have either known each other all your lives or have been waiting for each other all your lives. In love relationships, this codependent phase comes to a sudden halt when the couple stops, blinks, and asks, hey, who are you, and how did you get my cell number? If the couple can survive that abrupt ending to the codependent phase, they have a shot at having a serious, long-term relationship.

Alcoholics and addicts are notorious for having extremely poor boundaries. In other words, they're like that newborn child and mother or the couple that feels fused to the point of experiencing oneness at all times. In alcoholic relationships, there are no healthy boundaries. I don't have the dignity of making my own mistakes because you are too busy controlling, dictating, or rescuing me. You don't have a life of your own, because you're too busy managing mine. Instead of a relationship being a healthy, positive, nurturing dance of two souls, it's a cage match of struggle for control.

One of the benefits of Al-Anon is the development of healthy boundaries. Boundaries are limits on relationships. Think of the rubber divider in the supermarket check-out line that separates your groceries from those of the next shopper. If one of you doesn't put that boundary marker down, you'll get his rutabagas or he'll get your cat food. So the trick is to take that dividing stick and place it between the two sets of groceries so that everybody knows whose is whose.

We don't take that rubber divider and bop the other person over the head, shouting, "Hey, those are *my* kumquats!" Instead, you just place the boundary gently, and everybody knows which side of the line you are on. Al-Anon teaches people to place healthy boundaries, just like that supermarket checkout line divider, in their lives. You don't have a right to tell me what to do. I don't have a right to keep you from the consequences of your actions. I'm not going to pay for your addiction and I'm not going to bail you out of jail if that's where you land. We each are responsible for our own emotional well-being. And we establish those boundaries with the gentleness of a person placing the divider down on the checkout line. How do you do that? If I told you, you'd never go to Al-Anon. Go and find out for yourself.

7. *Recreation and Hobbies.*
There's a short piece of Al-Anon called "The Do's and Don'ts," which is read at many Al-Anon meetings. It's so simple, but often the wisest philosophies can be expressed in the fewest words. I'll share it with you here:

DO...

Forgive
Be honest with yourself
Be humble
Take it easy—Tension is harmful
Play—Find recreation and hobbies
Keep on trying whenever you fail
Learn all the facts about alcoholism
Attend Al-Anon meetings often
Pray

DON'T...

Be self-righteous

Try to dominate, nag, scold, or complain
Lose your temper
Try to push anyone but yourself
Keep bringing up the past
Keep checking up on the alcoholic
Wallow in self-pity
Make threats you don't intend to carry out
Be overprotective
Be a doormat[24]

Let's key in on one line that seems to have no connection with coping with addiction or alcoholism: *Find recreation and hobbies.* I'll explain the connection. Living with an alcoholic or addict, or being the adult child of one, can be so all-consuming that we forget that we actually have lives of our own. A woman at an Al-Anon meeting once said, "I know the slogan says *Live and let live.* I got good at letting other people live their lives. But I kept forgetting to live my own."

So along comes the gentle reminder, repeated in meeting after meeting, to find a recreation *of one's own.* You need to get out of the house. You need to do something for yourself. Go play *mah-jongg* with your friends. Go bowling or fishing. Take a course on improvisational comedy. Join a gym. But whatever you do, don't just sit there and allow the fact of addiction in your home to swallow you alive.

The Talmud tells over an idea of our sages, "In the future, a person will give a judgment and an accounting over everything that his eye saw and what he did not eat."[25] The idea is that we're supposed to *partake* of life and actually enjoy it.

---

24   Do's And Don'ts, © *2021 Al-Anon Family Groups, Inc.*
25   *Jerusalem Talmud Kiddushin,* 4:12:2-3

Trust me: "I didn't enjoy anything life has to offer because my son was an alcoholic" will probably not be an acceptable answer. Yes, it does take a lot of time and energy to cope with the alcoholism of a loved one. But while you're learning how, the suggestion is that you not let your own life pass you by.

8. *Usefulness.*

Newcomers to Al-Anon, or to any twelve-step fellowship for that matter, may feel as though they have nothing to offer. Everyone else seems to be so much more adept at handling the crises that the particular twelve-step fellowship they're encountering addresses. But time will pass and the newcomer will blossom as a result of regular attendance at Al-Anon meetings, taking the Steps with a sponsor, and ultimately working with others.

Think of Al-Anon as the chrysalis from which the caterpillar emerges as a beautiful butterfly. Indeed, the butterfly is a symbol of the Al-Anon fellowship. So there will come a time when you will be able to share all of your hard-won knowledge and experience in coping with an addict or alcoholic. You will be able to help the next person and alleviate his or her suffering. As it says in the *Big Book of Alcoholics Anonymous*, "Feelings of uselessness and self-pity will disappear."

You may not feel as though you have that much to offer right now, but the time will come, sooner or later, when your experience will benefit the next person. Many Al-Anon members report that being useful to others in this manner actually puts an entirely new spin on the pain and suffering they went through in living with an alcoholic or addict. Suddenly there's a real payoff—the ability to be truly useful to one's fellow man or woman. This is described in twelve-step literature as an experience that you don't want to miss.

9. *Detachment.*

In Al-Anon, there is no Step named "detachment." Instead, detachment is the reward that you receive for having taken the Twelve Steps and having worked a meaningful Al-Anon program. Detachment means that whatever the alcoholic or addict is doing or not doing, *it doesn't affect you.* A lofty goal, perhaps, but it's surprisingly attainable. Alcoholics and addicts are performance artists who need audiences. They need you to be participating in their destructive behavior. They need to see that you are horrified, shocked, angered, and generally miserable. If you're having a bad day, they're having a great day. When you can reach the point of detachment, you are no longer fueling the sick part of the addict or alcoholic that needs a dance partner.

There are different levels of detachment, of course. There's detachment with an axe, where I leave you and have nothing further to do with you. Sometimes, but not always, that's a necessary development. And then there's detachment with love, which is essentially where you say to the addict or alcoholic, "I'm sad that you're doing all this to yourself, but it's your choice. I'm not going to stand in your way. I love you, but I'm not going any more rounds with you or your disease." Detachment means a happier life for you, and it frequently means that the addict or alcoholic finally throws in the towel and says, "Fine. I'm not going to do this anymore. Let's get on with our lives."

10. *Serenity.*

Serenity means that I'm peaceful regardless of what's happening in the world around me. Can you be serene even though an addict or alcoholic is still drinking or using? Or died drinking or using? Amazingly, the answer is yes. But if you want to experience this for yourself, don't sit here reading this book. Instead, run, don't walk, to an Al-Anon meeting, which you can easily find by typing the phrase Al-Anon and the name of your city, county, or state into your friendly search engine.

You won't regret it.

CHAPTER 12

Spiritual Awakenings:
Three Who Are Changing Our World

A cross the United States, a handful of individuals and organizations have begun the hard work of destigmatizing addiction, alcoholism, and recovery in their Jewish communities. In most cases, the organizations or the individuals' dedication to this cause came into existence because of the addiction, recovery, or even the passing of a loved one. Let's now meet the leaders of three of these organizations, and get to know their perspectives on these challenging topics.

Lianne Forman, Executive Director, Communities Confronting Substance Use and Addiction

https://www.jewishccsa.org/

Lianne Forman discovered that her child was suffering from addiction. She and her family experienced tremendous isolation in their own journey. As a result, she and her husband founded *Communities Confronting Substance Use and Addiction* in order to help destigmatize addiction in her Jewish community of Teaneck, New Jersey, and beyond.

"Jewish communities have devoted serious attention to many important issues," Forman says. "There has been huge work done in the area of inclusion for developmentally disabled people, destigmatizing mental health issues, and other big topics. The reduction and ultimate eradication of the stigma surrounding substance misuse and addiction is the next major piece of our frontline agenda."

Forman eventually left her corporate law practice to focus on CCSA full-time. "It's not about if, but when," the CCSA website says. "We know it's just a matter of time before our children are exposed to drugs and alcohol if they haven't been already. Our programs are not about scaring our children, but teaching them that substances are dangerous to their developing brains and bodies. We teach them the facts, and help them develop refusal skills to make informed and healthy choices."

CCSA brings programming to schools in the form of youth prevention education, parent presentations, and faculty training programs, so as to help bring the issue of substance use and addiction into the open.

"We got serious pushback," Forman says, "when we wanted to bring programs into middle schools. People said, 'Isn't that a little young?' Our response is that kids of middle-school age frequently begin experimenting with drugs and alcohol while they are in middle school. We have to be aware of what's really going on, in order to help our children and our families.

"Kids that age are already exposed to alcohol and drugs. They see their parents making Kiddush on wine. They know about the opioid crisis. Did you ever teach your kid to look both ways before crossing the street? This is the same thing. We're just preparing them for the inevitable and helping them to make safe and healthy choices."

Forman also sees a strong connection between young people impacted by mental health issues and, perhaps, getting involved in drugs and alcohol and then ceasing to be religious.

"If you're not happy with yourself," she says, "looking at yourself in the mirror is painful, and knowing that God is watching is even worse. Religion requires so much introspection, which is all but impossible for people who can't sit in their own skin."

"Many of the kids who became addicts are no longer religious. They are interdating or intermarrying. Our goal is to allow those impacted by substance use and their families to come forward and get the help and communal support they need."

Forman says that she was invited to speak at the conference of Yeshiva University *rebbetzins*, or rabbis' wives. "They asked me, 'How should we treat addiction?' I told them, treat it like a family with any disease, like cancer. Do they need help with carpools? Meals? That removes the stigma and allows the family to talk about it openly, if they want to. It's a communal issue and deserves a communal response. So many people are struggling and ashamed to admit it."

Miriam Gisser, Recovery as Change

https://18forty.org/teshuva/

Miriam Gisser's first husband struggled with sobriety from drugs and alcohol, enjoying periods of "clean time" intermingled with retreats back into addiction. Over the course of that period, Gisser discovered Al-Anon. Ultimately, her husband succumbed to his drug addiction.

A teacher, Gisser has since remarried, and her quest in life is to bring the Al-Anon message to as many people as possible, especially in the Jewish community, where Al-Anon is not well known. She has a well-regarded podcast, *Recovery as Change*, on 18Forty, available on Apple Podcasts.

"After my husband passed," Gisser recalls, "my daughter, then nine years old, wanted to put his recovery keychains on her backpack as a way to remember her father. In Narcotics Anonymous, you get little keychains to symbolize getting thirty days clean, sixty days, and so on.

"The thought crossed my mind that if other people knew what the keychains meant, they would not let my daughter play with their children or let their kids come here. But I told her we could put her father's keychains on her backpack. It's a beautiful way to remember him, and to remind others that he succumbed to a disease, and that he wasn't a bad person."

Joseph Shamash, Beit T'shuvah

https://beittshuvah.org/

"Wherever we perform 'Freedom Song,'" Joseph Shamash says about Beit T'shuvah's signature performance piece, combining a Passover Seder with personal stories about addiction, people always come out and say, "That's me! I identify with that! That's my story, too!"

Shamash compares the process of recovery from addiction with Jews leaving Egypt. "They were getting out of slavery," he said, "getting out of their own way, in order to get to the promised land. That's what teshuvah is all about. It's about becoming whole and greater than what one was before."

That's the mission of Beit T'shuvah, a recovery house in Los Angeles. The house serves primarily Jewish clientele, including alcoholics and drug addicts, younger male "failure to launch" types in their twenties and early thirties, and what Shamash calls the "formerly frum."

"Eighty percent of the Hasidic world was wiped out during the Holocaust," Shamash notes, "so it only makes sense that post-traumatic stress disorder and trauma would be passed on inside their families. All Jewish communities, whether we're talking about the Persian community, YU Machmir, Chabad, or what have you, have a strong ethic involving success, education, family, and money. If you don't meet the criteria, you don't feel good about yourself. Also, the 'Facebook effect' creates a perception of other people having a perfect life compared with yours. This mitigates against recovery as well."

Shamash says that vulnerabilities are part of addiction. "Vulnerability wants to make us run and hide," he says, "like

Adam Ha-Rishon in the garden of Eden. But it's only through acknowledging our vulnerability that we have a chance to become strong."

***

These individuals and organizations are striving to chip away at the denial and the stigma surrounding addiction and recovery in the Jewish world. Reach out to them, support them, invite them to your community. Join them. The sages tell us, shockingly, that eighty percent of Jews perished during the ninth plague, the plague of darkness, with which God struck Egypt. Today, countless more Jews are perishing during our own modern plague of darkness—the ignorance that surrounds addiction and recovery in our world. Into that plague of darkness, these individuals and these entities are bringing much-needed, life-saving light.

CHAPTER 13

What Can We Do? What Must We Do?

Some people simply despise addicts and alcoholics or those associated with them. Worse, in our community, there is a state of indifference toward people with addictions. Nobody cares about them. If they slip off the side of the ark, it's just too bad. Indifference is worse than hate because hate implies some sort of connection or attachment. Indifference implies that the fate of the other person simply doesn't matter.

We don't all have to become addiction counselors. Yet we all share a responsibility to recognize that people from families with addiction, and addicts themselves, are human beings, and in our communities, they are our fellow Jews. We are commanded to love our fellow Jews and be responsible for our fellow Jews—we are all connected—instead of being indifferent or allowing them to just slip away. If there were more understanding and more support in the Orthodox Jewish community for such individuals and families, we would see far fewer people slip off the derech.

Our schools need to be better at handling those kids who don't come from "perfect" families. Our *shadchanim* or matchmakers need to have more compassion for such families, instead of marking them down and making it all but impossible for their children to find good matches. Our synagogues need to be more cognizant of the pervasiveness of alcohol culture. Is it necessary for the men to troop off to the janitor's closet during maftir to have a little schnapps? Just how boozy does the Shabbas morning Kiddush have to be?

Our institutions are simply reflections of ourselves. We need to stop pretending that being Jewish is some sort of shield, some sort of *Magen David*, against alcoholism and other forms of addiction. We have to snap out of our own community-wide denial and applaud the people who seek recovery, making it possible to do so without embarrassment or shame.

Likewise, we need to become accepting of the mistakes and different life journeys of people in our communities. Not everyone will carry a perfect track record. Does someone with a history of addiction, who has been solidly in recovery, not deserve to get married? Do children of an addict deserve to be stigmatized for a parent's past struggles? Forgiveness, which is at the heart of our relationship with God, has to be at the heart of our relationship with human beings as well.

We're never going to change the entire culture to the point where yichus, money, and community standing don't affect the way we see and measure families and individuals. It's human nature to pay attention to those things, as irrelevant as they may be when it comes to measuring the heart. But it's time, it's past time, to remove the stigma that surrounds addiction. It's time for understanding and compassion. It's time to end the ignorance about what recovery looks like, how it is attained, and why it is within the bounds of Judaism.

I told earlier the story about a well-known Alcoholics Anonymous speaker who, along with his brother, had gotten drunk in their car and woke up, after a blackout, in the middle of the city dump, into which they had unknowingly driven.

"They threw us away," one of the brothers said.

We live in a throwaway culture where we toss anything that isn't working perfectly, rather than try to repair it. We get rid of perfectly good cell phones simply because a new one comes out and it has a slightly better camera. But people aren't cell phones. We can't toss them away. As the novelist, Michael Connelly writes, "Unless everybody counts, nobody counts." Every aspect of the Jewish community must recognize that everybody counts...even those among us who suffer from or who come from families with problems of addiction.

We all count, and we all need to count.

So what can the Jewish community do right now to reduce or ideally eliminate the stigma surrounding alcoholism, addiction, and recovery? And how can we take steps to reduce addiction and make treatment more readily available for our community members? We'll start with simple steps and go to some ideas that will take considerably more time and effort to implement.

Treat Addiction as a Disease

Let's have more synagogues and temples follow the leads of those congregations that are already offering a *Mi Sheberach*, or prayer for the sick, for addicts and alcoholics each week. We are already praying for people to recover from every other illness. Why not addiction?

In the past several decades, society has chosen to view struggles with mental health as a form of "illness." The purpose of this language is not to imply that the issue can only be solved with medication. As with addiction—the solution is sometimes spiritual and sometimes psychological as well. Therapy, introspection, and self-awareness may be a part of the healing process. Still, we use the language of "illness" to teach us to stop judging people who are struggling with these issues. From the perspective of the person with mental illness, willpower just doesn't cut it. And we have to stop expecting it to.

Likewise, we need to treat addiction as a disease. If God forbid, a congregant comes down with a serious illness, the community supports him with meals, driving carpool, and other acts of *chesed*, or loving-kindness. Let's treat families of addicts with the same compassion and offer them the services that we already offer other members of the community suffering from illnesses that don't have such bad PR.

Increase Addiction Awareness

In our schools...

In our schools, let's step up drug and alcohol education from middle school on. Many alcoholics and addicts begin their drinking and using careers when still in middle school. So don't let anyone tell you that twelve-year-olds and thirteen-year-olds are too young to hear a message about addiction and recovery. Everything in society, and so much of Jewish culture, glamorizes and normalizes drinking. Isn't it time that they get the opposite message? One would hope so.

Many parents are hesitant to have their kids learn about things like addiction because they feel it is an assault on their children's innocence. They don't want their children to know about the stuff that's out there.

But if your child doesn't hear it from an adult, he or she is likely to hear it from other children at some point. And whose perspective would you prefer your child heard first?

In our communities...

Next, let's invite experts on addiction and recovery, as these concepts pertain to Jews and Judaism, as guest speakers in our religious institutions—our synagogues, temples, conventions, and schools. Let's inaugurate an annual "Recovery Shabbat" and invite a scholar-in-residence to give classes on the topic. This will both normalize the twelve-step recovery and destigmatize the problem of getting help.

Likewise, we need to make shuls safe places for addicts to seek help. We can do this in small ways by providing resources on the shul website inviting individuals struggling with addiction or their family members to reach out to the community rabbi, or directing them to nearby AA meetings. Likewise, we can print pamphlets that we keep available in shul about what to do if you know someone struggling with addiction and about the power of Al-Anon.

Again, none of these interventions need to be massive, expensive, or life-altering. We simply need to send the message that we are aware that addiction exists in our communities—we do not deny it—and will not make anyone ashamed for struggling with it, and we are ready and willing to do everything that we can to help.

Among our leaders...

To really be effective at providing support to addicts, our rabbis and community leaders *must understand the recovery process*. If someone reveals to a rabbi that he or she is struggling with an addiction, the response cannot be to pick up an extra study partner and learn some more Talmud.

In order to understand recovery, our leaders ought to attend AA, NA, and Al-Anon meetings, to see for themselves how the programs work. This way, they can effectively counsel their members in need of help.

Most rabbis are fascinated when they connect with twelve-step recovery meetings (if only because no one is talking in the back row, unlike in most synagogues!). Twelve-step members are always delighted to explain their programs to outsiders. Any rabbi from any denomination of Judaism who attends a twelve-step meeting will get a warm welcome from the members and will find a few people who will be happy to explain the ins and outs of getting clean. Rabbis and leaders who have made this effort will be infinitely better equipped to help their community members.

Host Meetings in More Jewish Spaces

Another way to combat denial and stigma within the Jewish community is by hosting more twelve-step meetings in synagogues and temples. That would send a dramatic message to our communities that addiction is real and that recovery is legitimate for Jews.

It doesn't take much to start a twelve-step meeting. The AA joke is that "all you need to start a new meeting is a resentment and a coffeepot." The resentment is about some other meeting you didn't like; the coffeepot is about, well, coffee, without which AA couldn't function. You don't really need resentment in this case—just an administrator at your local Jewish temple, synagogue, or community center willing to open the doors to the alcoholics and addicts who are living and dying nearby.

This will go a long way in showing that Jews and recovery can mix and that you don't necessarily have to go to churches to escape the clutches of booze, drugs, and other addictive substances and behaviors.

You can find AA meetings on beaches, in resort areas like Hawaii and Southern Florida all year long, and seasonally elsewhere. You'll find meetings on Capitol Hill in Washington DC, in Las Vegas casinos, and at an AA clubhouse in Times Square. See a Broadway show, grab a meeting. The perfect night in New York.

So if meetings take place in all these varied locations, why are so few situated in temples and synagogues? Some want to be careful about who comes into a temple or synagogue, for security reasons. We live in a time of intense anti-Semitism and terrorism, so allowing "just anyone" into a Jewish institution is a *prima facie* bad idea.

If security is a concern, we can look for ways to mitigate it—by having a community member trained in security protocols attend every meeting or keeping the meetings within the community to avoid the question of which outsiders to admit.

Why would it be so important to have meetings in temples and synagogues? A lot of Jews, especially observant Jews, find it very difficult to walk onto the grounds of a church, even more so if they are wearing a jacket and black hat. For religious Jews, this can be due to halachic reasons that potentially limit the permissibility of stepping into a church sanctuary, even though they may have permission from a rabbi to do so because taking this step will help save their lives. For less religious Jews, the memory of thousands of years of persecution and proselytizing might be a deterrent. Either way, it can be difficult for many Jews to set foot in the property. So, meetings in shuls might increase the likelihood of Jews actually seeking recovery.

If more temples and synagogues would host twelve-step meetings, it would also send a message to our communities: This is our problem, too. It's easy for Jews to fall back on the *"shiker iz a goy"* rationale and say that only non-Jews could be addicts or alcoholics. The presence of twelve-step meetings in temples and synagogues will go a long way toward rebutting that fallacious claim. We have to see that this is our problem, too. The goal is to normalize recovery in the Jewish community so that Jews in recovery are not treated as outliers or outsiders within their own world.

Cut Down On the Booze

In terms of helping prevent addiction or at least alcohol over-use, I think we need to consider cutting down on the amount of hard liquor that we serve at our celebratory events. A shot of schnapps is fine for most people, but is it healthy or neces-sary for anyone to drain several bottles of whiskey and vodka each week? What kind of message are we sending to our kids when they see a massive array of bottles of hard liquor avail-able, and consumed every Shabbat?

The default blessing at Kiddush is boray pri ha'gofen, which refers to wine and grape juice. Hard liquor is not tech-nically necessary for fulfilling any Shabbat commandment. If so, why are we making it easy, convenient, and legitimate for Jews with drinking problems to get loaded? Along the same lines, let's reconsider the Ritual Committee, the little drink-ing gatherings that take place in the boardroom, or the jan-itor's room during the reading of the Haftorah. If we don't want our kids to drink or use in secret, why do we allow the adults? Maybe these drinking groups need to be made both more moderate and more public. Maybe they don't need to happen at all?

At the risk of being a wet blanket, while we are on this subject, I have to bring up alcohol on Simchat Torah and Purim. One alcoholic I spoke with said that he drank enough alcohol on Purim to kill an elephant. Was he drinking that much the rest of the week? Not surprisingly, the answer is no.

It's true, for people without issues with alcohol, drinking on these days can add some level of joy and exuberance. But for anyone who is challenged by booze, and for teenagers as well, both holidays often become an excuse for dangerous levels of consumption. How many times have you heard about the teenage boys who spent Simchat Torah night vomiting in the alley behind the shul? Is that where you want your own son to be?

We don't need to eliminate alcohol from these occasions, but we do need to reduce it dramatically. There is no reason to provide enough alcohol to allow the entire shul to get dangerously drunk. Buy fewer bottles, and have someone be responsible for pouring. And put the extra few hundred bucks toward a more lavish Kiddush or meal. It's a win-win situation. Oh...and maybe don't serve the alcohol to under-twenty-ones?

Remove the Shame from Recovery

Ultimately, the goal of this book is to demand that the Jewish community look its addiction problem in the face and stop denying that addiction is among us. It is also to force us to realize that the shame that we attach to addiction is drowning our addicts rather than helping them. Shame is forcing families and individuals into silence because they are afraid of the repercussions of speaking up. It is holding people back from seeking the help they need.

To confront this, we need to remove the shame from addiction and recovery. Like any other illness, we need to treat it matter-of-factly, without judgment or condemnation. It should not besmirch a family when applying to a Jewish school. It should not besmirch a family when joining a synagogue. It should not besmirch a family seeking a marriage match for a child. Right now, families are terrified to admit that any family member is in recovery for fear of destroying the chances for a son or daughter to make a match. What if this weren't the case? What if we stopped shaming individuals who are in recovery and instead celebrated them?

Okay, we don't have to make them honorees of dinners (where more wine flows), but let's not penalize people who are working so hard to turn their lives around. Obviously, this last suggestion is a major cultural shift, and it won't happen easily. But at least we can put it on the table.

Likewise, we need to give platforms to recovered addicts and their parents and family members to speak about their experiences out loud and in public. An addict is allowed to break his own anonymity if he chooses. By speaking his story out loud, he gives others the opportunity to step up and do the same. At the same time, he can share what helped and what hurt. His family can explain what they needed from the community to pull through the tough times.

When we break the silence, no-talk rules fall away. Everyone has skeletons in the closet. We should not live in fear of having them discovered. Rather, we should use them to connect with others struggling with the same things. We should use them to remind us that in every person's life, there are experiences of slavery and redemption. And there is no shame in that.

***

So there we have it. A menu of actions we can take immediately that can reduce the effects of alcoholism and addiction in our community and make it legitimate for folks to find a way to get and stay sober. How much longer will individuals and communities suffer in silence? How many more people like my friend David must we bury due to drug or alcohol abuse, and how many homes must be destroyed because we were too timid to understand and destigmatize alcoholism and addiction?

If not us, then who? And if not now, when?

ACKNOWLEDGMENTS

First, while many people assisted in making this book happen, all errors and misstatements are my own. That said...

My publishers, David Bernstein and Adam Bellow, believed in this project from our first conversation about it. Gentlemen, thank you for your continuing faith in me.

Aleigha Kely did a phenomenal job managing all the details. So grateful to you!

Emunah Fialkoff gave the manuscript a very thorough top-to-bottom edit. Without her brilliance, this book would never have had a chance.

Rabbi Ari Zahtz of Yeshiva University and my congregation, B'nai Yeshurun of Teaneck, gave me excellent notes and kept me from making some big blunders in print. He took a lot of time to go painstakingly through the manuscript and point out nuances (and outright errors) that I hadn't recognized. Thank you, Rabbi Zahtz!

David A., the person I described briefly at the opening of the book, was a wonderful, kind and sweet person who didn't deserve the drug addiction that took his life. He was a devoted friend and left behind a devastated family and community. My friendship with him, as I wrote, prompted me to become a volunteer counselor to addicts and families. I'm hoping that this book, which is a tribute to his life, inspires others to take action—to get clean and sober, to recognize what their alcoholic or addicted family members are really dealing with, and to create space in the Jewish community for people in recovery. If that happens, then maybe, just maybe, David didn't die in vain.

ABOUT THE AUTHOR

N
ew York Times bestselling author Michael Levin has written, cowritten, or edited more than twenty national bestsellers and is an accomplished journalist who has written for top outlets including the *New York Times*, the *Wall Street Journal*, *HuffPost*, the *Los Angeles Times*, and the *Jerusalem Post*. He runs www.MichaelLevinWrites.com, a ghostwriting company. Michael is the co-author of *Lift Your Voice: How My Nephew George Floyd's Murder Changed the World* by Angela Harrelson.